— THE —
GENEROSITY
MINDSET

A JOURNEY TO
BUSINESS SUCCESS BY RAISING
YOUR CONFIDENCE, VALUE, AND PRICES

JOHN RAY

Published by:
ELITE ONLINE PUBLISHING
63 East 11400 South
Suite #230
Sandy, UT 84070
EliteOnlinePublishing.com

275 S. Main Street
Alpharetta, GA 30009
john@johnray.co

Editing and publishing support provided by The Write Image Consulting, LLC and Write Your Life.

ISBN: 978-1-961801-29-5
ISBN: 978-1-961801-19-6
LCCN: 2023923289

BUS060000 BUSINESS & ECONOMICS / Small Business
BUS025000 BUSINESS & ECONOMICS / Entrepreneurship

QUANTITY PURCHASES: Schools, companies, professional groups, clubs, and other organizations may qualify for special terms when ordering quantities of this title. For information, email john@johnray.co

BONUS

You can find the resources mentioned in this book and additional information at www.thegenerositymindset.com/bookresources.

For my wife, Monica.
This book is a direct result of her constant support,
generosity, and love.

For my parents, John and Phyllis,
who set me on a path of service and have lived
what they taught.

TABLE OF CONTENTS

INTRODUCTION

Several years ago, I was on a discovery call with a videographer. This man had been in business for five years, and he knew he needed to make some major changes to his business if he was going to achieve the goals he had set for himself.

He was proud of the progress he had made with his business over the years, which was notable, and he was ready to take it to another level. Something, however, was holding him back from earning the revenue he wanted. He described his services and some of the clients he worked with. He wanted to work with more "best fit" clients, and he was in a quandary as to how to move forward.

This videographer ran through several issues and concerns he felt were affecting his business negatively. As he did, he unknowingly checked off just about every red flag I look for when assessing the pricing of professional services providers.

About twenty minutes into the conversation, I said, "I can tell your pricing is too low."

He was shocked, and I understood why.

"How do you know that?" he asked. "I haven't told you my prices yet."

"In no particular order, there are several reasons," I replied. "First, you price by the hour. By definition, a professional services provider like you who prices by the hour is underpricing their services.

"Second, you tell me that all clients are paying the same price. Not all clients have the same values. Different clients value your services differently. You probably go the extra mile for clients who don't value that added care you're giving them, and you give them way too much for what you're charging. You also probably have a few clients who would be willing to pay you much more than you are charging them. They love you, your work, and how you do what you do."

By this point, I could tell he had begun mentally scratching his head and wondering how I was able to diagnose his situation so quickly. I continued.

"Third, you're not offering options. Options are a powerful way to tailor your services to your best-fit clients who love what you accomplish for them, and they're willing to pay you a good price for that."

He interrupted, "But options seem like too much trouble. One price is easier for me to keep track of. It's also most fair to my clients."

When I explained that a pricing structure for his services is just as important to his clients as it is to him—even more so in most cases— he settled down and listened to the rest of what I had to share.

"Fourth, you complain that you feel like you're working too hard for too little money. For professional services providers like you, that's always a sign of a pricing problem."

Should I let this guy off the hook now or keep going? I wondered. He seemed to be taking it all in fairly well. So with two final points, I concluded the diagnosis.

"Fifth, you seem to be taking on most projects which come your way. More prospects should be turning you down because of price."

"Turning me down?" he asked.

"Yes, and we can talk more about why later," I said. "Finally, you're talking too much about you, what and how you do what you do, instead of the challenges clients have that you solve for them. What that tells me is you're not having deeper value conversations with clients at all. A value conversation is the dialogue you must have with a prospective client to understand the difficulties you help them overcome. If you persuasively articulate how your solution to their problems moves the needle for their business and for themselves personally, then you'll be able to set better prices."

I paused. It was a lot for him to digest all at once.

Finally, his silence gave way to a hopeful "aha." I knew he could see the possibilities of making some changes.

"You're exactly right," he said. "I need to work on my pricing."

And so his transformative journey began.

In the four-plus decades in which I have served variously as a Wall Street analyst, an investment banker, an investment manager, and a business consultant, I've learned firsthand what famed investor Warren Buffett once said about pricing: "The single, most important decision in evaluating a business is pricing power. If you've got the power to raise prices without losing business to a competitor, you've got a very good business. And if you have to have a prayer session before raising the price by ten percent, then you've got a terrible business." Over the past twelve years, as I have worked exclusively with small businesses—specifically solo and small firm professional services providers—I have affirmed the idea that the difference between a very good business and a terrible one often comes down to pricing.. This truth, however, comes with a couple of twists.

With an enterprise company, pricing starts with marketing studies, competitive analyses, policies, cost accounting, coordination between marketing and sales departments, and endless committee meetings. As a services provider, essentially selling your "grey matter," you are the product. You are not pricing an inanimate object like doggie treats, a decorated cake, or a garden tool. You are pricing your knowledge and your experience. You are pricing yourself. It's an intimate, highly personal action.

Consequently, your mindset often becomes a major issue. Some of those mindsets can be injurious to your ability to price your services effectively and, by extension, to the rest of the business.

Further, most entrepreneurs go into business without much, if any, formal training in pricing. Assuming you went to business school or majored in business in college, you are in the minority if you took a single course in pricing. Therefore, your ability to price your work relative to the value it generates for your clients is limited.

The common goal of all services providers I've ever met is to do transformative work for clients who they love working with and to get paid commensurate with the value they deliver to those clients. For you to get to that point in your own business, though, you must adopt a different mindset that can replace those mindsets which inhibit your growth. You must be able to diagnose and communicate the value you deliver to clients, and, in turn, more effectively price to receive a portion of that value.

In truth, there is nothing proprietary about my work on value and pricing. The concepts I teach, write about, and present in workshops are all out there, somewhere, on Google, in books, in presentations on LinkedIn Learning, in research papers. So why, then, are folks seemingly irrational enough to pay me good money for one-on-one coaching or to conduct a workshop on value and pricing? Why would they pay me when all that information is out there somewhere and they could go find it themselves?

My clients—primarily solopreneur services providers—hire me to gather the plethora of information that exists on value and pricing. This includes the studies, books, ideas, and concepts that would take them years to sift through, understand, and apply. With my guidance, they learn the techniques I have spent decades gaining insight into and practicing, and they get my support as they apply those techniques to transform their businesses.

Beyond the "how to," though, my clients start to recognize and modify the mindsets that have held them back from sustainable success. They replace those mindsets with a powerful way to serve their clients with what I call The Generosity Mindset.

These solopreneurs have critical changes they need to make in their business, and they need help today. They need to build a successful practice today. Therefore, they don't have time to do all the work, the reading, and the research, nor do they want to determine what part of all that works for them and their business, and what doesn't.

I get hired because I shortcut a client's learning process significantly, saving them a ton of time and a mountain of effort. Such clients have grown weary of other approaches to their problems and are urgently seeking the benefits that come from solving those problems.

Beyond saving folks time and effort, there are other reasons I get hired. Clients hire me because I'm able to explain complex concepts with stories and metaphors that make those concepts come alive for them. They engage me because I'm willing to listen to their problems and address them directly. They work with me because I have a reputation for delivering much more value than the price they pay. All those reasons I get hired are based on the value others see in me, value which is intrinsic to me and not my content. The same is true for you.

Whether you are a consultant or a coach, marketing or branding professional, business advisor, attorney, CPA, or in virtually any other professional services discipline, your content, your technical expertise, is not unique. None of us wants to believe that, but deep down, if we're honest with ourselves, we know it's true.

What is proprietary, though, is your experience and how you synthesize and deliver what you know. What's special is your demeanor or the way you deal with your best-fit clients. What's invaluable is how you deliver great value by guiding people through massive changes in their personal life and in their business that bring them to a place they never thought possible.

The combination of all these elements is quite different for you compared to any other services provider in your industry (otherwise known as your competitors). You have a combination of tangibles and intangibles uniquely yours, a combination that appeals to a particular swath of clients. Some clients are attracted to your onboarding process, while others appreciate the education you provide them throughout their work with you. Some like your follow up, the resources you provide, the support team you work with, your accessibility, or the intuitive way you anticipate their needs. Each of these characteristics makes you unique and adds value to the client experience, a value you must learn to put a price on.

You may be a solopreneur in the strictest sense of the word—it's just you as the "chief cook and bottle washer" of your business. You might have grown, and are now using a virtual assistant, contractor labor, or even have employees. Maybe you have taken on a partner to perform the technical work involved in your practice. Whatever the case, you are the founder of the business, and you are both the chief professional who delivers services as well as the chief (and most likely the only) salesperson. Success or failure in building a sustainable practice falls on you. Wherever you are in your journey, the term "solopreneur" applies, so I'll use it throughout this book.

If pricing your value feels uncomfortable or unfamiliar to you, keep reading. You're about to learn why putting a price on the value you provide your clients serves them and you . . . and you'll learn the factors involved in getting your price right. So let's take this journey together.

PART 1

GET THE RIGHT MINDSET ABOUT VALUE

CHAPTER 1

THE MINDSETS THAT HOLD YOU BACK

The great part about being a professional services provider is that you carry the factory floor around every day. It's between your ears, and it's yours and yours alone. You don't need an expensive, fancy building or facility to operate in. You don't necessarily need a lot of employees—or any, if you prefer to work solo.

You control the quality and delivery of the service. You can adjust the service on the fly. You also control whether you deliver it or not and even who you allow to buy your service.

The product is you, not an inanimate, third-party object like a coffee machine or an automobile. The product—your expertise, experience, and advice—is all in your head.

You are the product, and that simple fact makes your work highly personal.

From the client's perspective, there is no psychological separation between you and the product. When a new client agrees to purchase your services, in a sense, they are buying a part of you. When a client comments on the quality of your work, or lack thereof, your senses are heightened because those comments may be very personal. When a client fires you or a prospect turns you down, it feels personal. You feel rejected.

Because your factory floor is between your ears, your business is affected by your mindsets, whether positive or negative. You have carried some of these mindsets around for as long as you can remember. You may have developed some of them as a child. You might have a vague sense of what's going on in your head and how it affects your business, or you might not have any idea that you're carrying some of these mindsets and how they might be affecting you and your business.

The success of your professional services practice depends on the mindsets you allow to dominate your thinking. Your mindset about your business—and there are many mindsets you could adopt—is the foundation of everything, and certainly the key to your success. That goes for everything in your business, from your business model, your positioning, prospecting, sales conversations, marketing, delivery, follow up, and, in particular, your pricing.

Contrary to pricing a product like doggie treats, when you price your services, that pricing often gets quite personal. You are essentially pricing yourself, and that can be very uncomfortable. No one wants to put an actual price tag on themselves. The difference between how a bag of doggie treats is priced and the pricing of your services often boils down to mindset. Because your mindset affects how you view yourself, it can heavily influence how you price your services. Your pricing, in turn, has serious implications on not just your profitability, but also on your positioning with clients.

Price is a marketing signal. Depending on how they are set, your prices can be a signal of either quality or inferiority. Pricing, therefore, affects the perception clients have of both your expertise and the quality of your services.

There are several mindsets a solopreneur can assume, some of which I will discuss here. A few are more common than others, and you may identify yourself in one or even a number of these mindsets:

- The Mindset of Inadequacy
- The Mindset of an Imposter
- The Mindset of Comparison
- The Mindset of Helping
- The Mindset of Scarcity

It is important to identify those mindsets that hold you back as you build a successful professional services practice and then develop the right approach to eliminate destructive thinking patterns.

The Mindset of Inadequacy ("I'm not good enough.")

This mindset might be the most common of all the mindsets that inhibit your professional and personal growth. The mindset of inadequacy is a pervasive belief that you are simply not good enough or that you do not have the skills or experience you need to thrive in your practice. This mindset is not the same as imposter syndrome, in which you think you are somehow deceiving others. With the mindset of inadequacy, you believe that you are missing some of the competence you need to elevate the quality of the clients you work with.

The way you run your business is a dead giveaway for the mindset of inadequacy. You might be reluctant to promote yourself due to a fear of being exposed as "not good enough." Maybe you don't take on engagements or clients that seem too challenging because you prefer to stay inside the comfort zone you currently occupy. Because you fear that clients will not see the value, you might be reluctant to set prices which adequately reflect that value.

The mindset of inadequacy can be particularly pervasive early in the life of your business. You think that because your business is brand new, you haven't proven yourself, and therefore you cannot go after certain clients that are too large or too established for you. Your pricing is affected because you feel like you must discount your services simply because you are just starting your business.

When you actually do get clients, the mindset of inadequacy shows up in how you interact with them. You might minimize your own abilities or accomplishments despite the positive comments others say about you. Relatedly, you consistently refuse to accept praise for the quality of your work. You rush to dismiss compliments, deflecting that praise by saying "Anyone could do it" or "I got lucky" or some other self-deprecating response.

You might avoid certain networking groups and events, industry associations, or conferences because you feel you're "not good enough" right now. A mindset of inadequacy causes you to spend excessive amounts of time preparing for client meetings or presentations because you fear you'll be uncovered as being not ready or even incompetent.

A need for validation of your work might indicate that you have a mindset of inadequacy. Repeatedly seeking confirmation from mentors, clients, or your peers, even though you produce quality work, may be a sign of this mindset.

When it comes to pricing, a mindset of inadequacy reveals itself in a particularly lethal way. In this case, you charge less than you might otherwise even consider, or you are quick to give discounts because down deep you question how much your services are worth. The impact on your business may be quite direct, and injuriously so. You might avoid challenging yourself to pursue clients who are a great fit for you and different market niches which you clearly have the capability to service. You miss out on partnerships or collaborations with strategic partners because the inadequacies you inflate in your head might expose you. These evasive maneuvers can limit your capacity to add new clients and to expand your business.

When your mindset of inadequacy leads to over-preparation, you work much longer hours than needed. You avoid vacations because you believe you don't deserve the time off, instead of viewing time away from your business as a crucial aspect of self-care. Your productivity declines and you might have symptoms of a mild depression or worse. At the extreme, you could experience burnout and problems at home.

Finally, because you diminish the value of your services and give signals to clients that you're doing so, you stain your reputation. You are perceived as the cheap or discount provider in your field or niche. Clients sense your lack of confidence, which causes them to avoid you in favor of other providers. The clients you do have are the most price-sensitive clients, those attracted to you because all they care about is the lowest price. Such clients are inevitably the most demanding because they don't want to pay a fair price for the services they eagerly consume.

The resulting financial strain becomes quite difficult. You feel like you are working too hard for too little money. You may be making money, but in truth you only are profitable because you don't factor in the value of your time or other inputs into your business. If you priced the value of your time, you would be unprofitable.

All these factors get you into a vicious mental cycle, fueling and seemingly confirming your mindset of inadequacy.

The Mindset of an Imposter ("I'm a fraud.")

The mindset of an imposter, more commonly known as imposter syndrome, is your internal belief, against all objective evidence to the contrary, that your achievements and successes are somehow the result of something other than your talents and experience. Any success you have must have been gained accidentally through luck or timing because otherwise you are a fraud. You fear someone asking you a question or putting you in a position where you will be exposed for who you really are.

The effects on your business are similar to what can occur with the mindset of inadequacy. You feel like you must work especially hard to compensate for the real you and to keep up the façade. You avoid new opportunities with clients and resist scaling your business because you don't believe you will be able to keep up the act. You hesitate or entirely avoid showcasing your work and your successes because such "bragging" might cause someone to point you out as an imposter.

Many of the same behavioral tendencies resulting from an inadequacy mindset also pop up with imposter syndrome. You may question your own capabilities as a professional in your given field, despite plenty of objective evidence to the contrary. This recurring self-doubt causes you to discount your own skills and capabilities, believing any success you have is simply luck or timing. Your fear of failure leads you to risk aversion. You are stuck in paralysis by analysis. Your mental certainty that the faker in you will suddenly spill out in front of others causes you to feel insecure and out of place, especially when you are among your peers or leaders in your industry. Even though your work is consistently excellent, you possess an inordinately strong desire to have others validate the quality of your services.

The resulting effect on your business can be quite stifling. Your opportunities to grow are limited because you hesitate to take on new challenges presented by more complex clients that often represent greater fees to you. You don't pursue ideal clients because you have convinced yourself that they would never hire you. Your professional network of strategic referral partners is stale and limited. You avoid upgrading your network of connections or collaborations that might be fruitful because you fear you're just not that good.

You can't take actions which should be easy decisions because you fear making mistakes that could expose you as a fraud. You are inefficient with your time, as you over-prepare and redo your work multiple times. You over-edit your client communications and content marketing pieces such as blogs or social media posts. Finally, your mental well-being may be worn down by the constant fear and anxiousness of being found out. The mental and emotional strain may directly inhibit your business as well as affect your personal well-being.

The value and pricing implications of the mindset of an imposter can be severe. You do not recognize your own value as a professional services provider, despite all evidence to the contrary, because underneath it all you think you are a fake. Because you don't recognize your own value, your ability to communicate that value to others is severely hampered. When it comes to pricing your services, you consistently undercharge because you don't believe you deserve a higher price. As with the mindset of inadequacy, with the mindset of an imposter, your ineffectiveness in pricing leads to poor marketing results, signaling to clients that your work is inferior.

The Mindset of Comparison ("I'm not as good as . . .")

The mindset of comparison involves continuously measuring your own abilities, successes, and ultimately your worth as a services provider against the abilities, successes, and worth that you *perceive* in others. While some comparison can be motivating, excessively judging yourself by your peers can inflame existing feelings of inadequacy and imposter syndrome. Further, the mindset of comparison can lead to jealousy and unwarranted dissatisfaction with yourself and your business.

A note on my use and emphasis of the word "perceive." The mindset of comparison is an epidemic in today's digital world, where those you view as competitors, as well as your peers, are constantly showcasing the best of themselves on social media. The notion that their success is eclipsing yours is a perception fueled by slick social media posts. The reality, if you really knew it, would cure your mindset of comparison. You continue to doom scroll on your social media feeds, though, glossing over what you intuitively know—that every business has its own unique journey, full of challenges, problems, and failures.

Your comparison may be completely wrong and therefore leading you to faulty assumptions and insecurities. For instance, you might compare yourself to someone who is scaling their business with employees and contractors, while you are perfectly content with your solo, home-based business. Both choices are equally valid and based on the preferences of the respective business owners. Your mistake is comparing yourself to a business owner who may seem comparable, but who in fact is pursuing an entirely different scaling strategy than you are.

Further manifestations of the mindset of comparison in your business can include shifting your business strategy in response to what you perceive others are doing and away from your own well-conceived business strategy and direction. Instead of celebrating others and their successes, which can bolster relationships that help your business down the road, your feelings of inadequacy are stoked. Such may be the case even if your business is otherwise performing quite well.

Your behavior can be bent in destructive ways by an unhealthy comparison mindset. You may be focused on external metrics, which have more to do with your competitors or how you perceive them through their social media posts, than on your own business needs. For example, you may be envious of the number of LinkedIn connections your peers possess, forgetting that you serve a niche which is highly specialized, many of whom may not even be active on LinkedIn.

You may frequently change your tactics to counter those of others when such tactics are not a fit with the overall strategy for your business. You might be copying or imitating strategies, particular services, marketing initiatives, or branding which you perceive (there's that word again) cause others to outperform you. Such a comparison may be totally unwarranted.

You may develop envy and jealousy, which might simmer under the surface. If expressed, such feelings may cause you to make assumptions about how others have it easier than you do, or they somehow have all the luck. You might make negative social media posts aimed at those you are envious of, rather than positive posts to attract your target client.

Ultimately, your mindset of comparison may cause chronic dissatisfaction with your business that is completely out of line based on any objective measure. You minimize even those successes of yours which are quite remarkable.

The impact on your business can be significant. That unique value proposition which you have carefully honed through trial and error over the years might erode as you shift in your client acquisition tactics to mirror others. Your clients and strategic referral partners who want to refer you may be confused and put off by a changing brand voice. You might be investing in what's popular instead of what's been proven effective for your unique business.

In terms of value and pricing issues, a mindset of comparison may cause destructive distortions. Thinking again about your value proposition, your dilution of brand identity as you stray from the value you have already identified affects whether clients continue to be attracted to you. Further, you may start attracting the wrong clients, and your ability to justify your premium pricing may go out the window. You might be more eager to discount because you want to outperform or one-up someone else.

As you compare yourself to others, particularly those who are at a different place in their business journey than you are, you might mistakenly judge your own business by the perceptions of others. You might undervalue and therefore underprice your own services. You may become convinced that you need to discount your services to match what you perceive others are doing.

The Mindset of Helping ("I want to help everyone.")

You are a services professional. You serve others, and you are motivated to serve using the expertise and experience you have developed over many years. You are on a mission. It's a problem, though, when you take your mission so seriously that you allow the following statement to come out of your mouth: "I just want to help everyone."

I see this particularly in solopreneurs for whom the new car smell of their business hasn't worn off yet. (Larger firms do not have this problem. That is one reason they are larger.) Their enthusiasm for their business is so buoyant that everywhere they look, they see someone who needs their services. They are the proverbial hammer that only sees nails, always and everywhere. Although such an intention may be noble, the mindset of helping blurs the lines between genuine service to others and overextending yourself in ways that challenge your positioning and your ability to deliver the outcomes you promise.

The mindset of helping shows up in your business in several ways. You take every client or project that comes your way. You are hesitant to specialize because you fear you might exclude potential clients. Scope creep is a common theme in your work with clients. Even when client requests do not match either your expertise or your capacity to adequately serve, you agree to them anyway because you're just here to help.

The resulting behaviors you exhibit include branding and messaging yourself and your business in ways that are broad as you attempt to appeal to everyone. You overcommit to an aimless array of clients. You never say no to a new client, even if you know down deep that they are not a good fit for your business.

The impact on your business is severe. Because you accept all comers, you have clients who cannot pay you adequately for your services or sometimes not at all. You are stretched thin trying to work on projects that are outside your core expertise and comfort zone. The irony of the helping mindset is that when an ideal client fit appears, you are so busy that you don't have time to work with them or even pitch them.

Here is one of the biggest dangers of the mindset of helping, both for you and your clients: Taken to an extreme, this mindset will cause you to resent your clients. You see them as the cause of how hard you are working for as little revenue as you're earning. You will gradually find yourself grinding your teeth when you see them on your phone's caller ID. You will take too long to return their calls, and you'll be short with them when you talk to them. At its extreme, the mindset of helping has the exact opposite effect of where such a noble intention started. You aren't helping your clients, and you're not helping your business or yourself.

The Mindset of Scarcity ("It's either me or you.")

The underpinning of the mindset of scarcity is the belief that the universe is limited and that the pie of opportunity is fixed. There are not enough clients and revenue to go around, such that if you gain a client that opportunity has been taken away from everyone else. To put it colloquially, if you are affected by the mindset of scarcity, you believe that it's a dog-eat-dog world and that you must constantly avoid wearing doggie treat underwear.

A mindset of scarcity causes you to see everyone as the competition, even professionals whose expertise is tangential to yours with little overlap. You are reluctant to share your knowledge or collaborate with your peers in any way. You resent anyone in a similar industry who comes into "your territory" in your local Chamber, networking group, or association. You immediately regard them as threats. When that happens, your insecurities are heightened. You resist any dialogue with others whatsoever, forgoing possible strategic partnerships and referral partners who could help your business. You don't want to take the chance. If you're not already doing it because of another mindset we've discussed, you accept engagements or clients who are not the right fit because you fear you'll miss out on what you consider to be limited revenue opportunities.

You fail to recognize or refuse to acknowledge that the world is an abundant ecosystem with opportunities for growth being created in every corner of the marketplace of ideas and commerce. You may have grown up in an environment of economic need, or you may be influenced by the idea that money is inherently evil. Whatever your background, your default is worry—about money, having enough clients to sustain your business, client retention, or other so-called competitors.

Whatever the cause of your mindset of scarcity, it restrains your business in a variety of ways. When you are sitting in front of prospective clients, you come across as needy or overly aggressive because your mentality is driven by a fear of loss. You reek of the "stench of desperation." The prospect can smell it, and it scares them away from you. When that happens, you are quick to offer discounts, which makes the stench even more foul-smelling. Your ability to build trust, the essential fuel for any professional services business, is gone.

You don't have the amount or quality of referrals you would like because potential strategic referral partners see that it's a one-way street with you. You are only focused on yourself, and you don't see how boosting others can help your business.

When clients do come your way, you take on more business than you can handle at the wrong pricing because you don't trust the abundance of the market enough. The only criterion for whether someone is a good fit client is that their check clears. The result of all of this is that the quality of your service suffers, and so does your reputation.

We have covered several mindsets that hold you back in your business as a services provider. These mindsets keep you from growing your business, adding clients you love working with who are a great fit for your practice, and pricing at levels that reflect the value of the outcomes you can deliver.

The great news for you is that mindsets can be changed, even the negative ones you think are cemented in the very fiber of who you are as a human being.

Mindsets Can Be Changed

"Mindsets are not set in stone. They are just beliefs, and beliefs can be changed."

~Carol S. Dweck, PhD, in
Mindset: The New Psychology of Success

Depending on your makeup and how deep-seated some of these mindsets might be, you may need to do deeper inner work. I have done this work many times with clients who need to establish a better mindset to counter the negative ones holding them back. You need a mindset that will help you attract better clients and achieve better pricing for your business. You need a mindset that will help you restore joy to your business. You need a mindset that supports the very core of why you started your business in the first place. That is The Generosity Mindset.

CHAPTER 2

THE GENEROSITY MINDSET

There is a long-held belief that dominates the minds of many professional services providers and keeps many solopreneurs struggling, frustrated, and lacking in their business growth: "I should get paid what I'm worth."

If your first thought after reading that statement is, "Well, yeah, of course. I completely agree," I implore you to continue reading to find out why this belief is causing you to lose business.

Your own definition of value, what you think you are worth, is irrelevant to clients and prospects. It creates a false crutch of confidence that can be snatched from beneath you with no warning. That confidence crutch you have created over your time in business has you thinking that the amount you charge for your services is in direct proportion to the amount of time you devote to acquire and service your clients, plus all the years of experience you gained from a previous job or other clients, plus the level of care and concern you put into each project. Here's a secret: Your clients don't care about any of that.

I don't disagree that you should get paid what you're worth, or I wouldn't have written this book. The problem with this thinking is that it is usually based entirely on your own opinion of yourself, the services provider. Your opinion of yourself, in turn, is formed by the mindsets that dominate your thinking.

"What I'm worth" is dangerous language for you. Such thinking keeps a focus on you, and in turn, whatever combination of mindsets mentioned in the previous chapter which are holding you back. These mindsets, whether of inadequacy or scarcity or others, can cause "what I'm worth" to easily morph into thoughts of "what I need" or "what I deserve." At an extreme, "what I'm worth" can justify taking advantage of people. What you need, or think you deserve, is irrelevant. The only thing that is relevant is how clients value the solutions you provide to their problems.

There is a better way to know your value. It runs counter to much of what is celebrated in today's business world. It is so paradoxical that it may seem too idealistic or too good to be true.

It is The Generosity Mindset.

If you adopt and consistently practice this mindset, you will unleash a powerful antidote to the mindsets that hold you back. Moreover—and here is the most counterintuitive aspect of The Generosity Mindset—you will make more money in your practice than you ever thought was possible, and you will have a more joyful life.

What is The Generosity Mindset?

The Generosity Mindset is one that is selflessly focused on others and their needs first. It is one in which your desires and goals take a backseat, but only temporarily.

The Generosity Mindset is living confidently in the expectation that service to others will rebound to you. Part of the joy of life with this mindset is living with the expectation that the universe is an abundant ecosystem, and that the generosity you practice today will come back to you in ways you cannot even begin to imagine.

In business, adopting The Generosity Mindset means cultivating within yourself a spirit of empathy, compassion, and collaboration with others. The Generosity Mindset involves a genuine investment in the success and happiness of not only your clients, but of your employees, partners, and even competitors. Instead of solely focusing first on your own personal success, you begin to view your network as a place you unselfishly seek to uplift and empower others to thrive. You wake up each morning seeking to be a source of support, encouragement, and inspiration for all who you encounter, without calculating how those individuals may benefit you. Embracing this mindset transcends the boundaries of your business. It extends to all aspects of your life: to your family, your neighborhood and larger community, and society and the world as a whole.

While The Generosity Mindset may seem counterintuitive to achieving personal success, it is paradoxically the key to unlocking deep and lasting prosperity. By genuinely putting others first, you create for yourself a virtuous cycle of trust, influence, goodwill, and reciprocity. The universe responds in kind. You will be able to open doors to new opportunities, form valuable and unexpected alliances, and propel you and your business toward and even past the goals you have set for yourself.

There is nothing new or novel about The Generosity Mindset. It is my own language and methods for referring to ancient wisdom and even more modern business sageness that spans across cultures and geography.

In the Jewish tradition, generosity is a central theme deeply rooted in the teachings of the Torah (the first five books of the Hebrew Bible) and further developed in later rabbinic literature. The Torah, for example, instructs farmers to leave the corners of their field unharvested for the poor to harvest themselves. Debts were to be forgiven in the Sabbatical year, once every seven years, and in the Jubilee year, every fifty years following seven sets of seven years (49).

Generosity is also a recurring tenet of the teachings of Jesus Christ. Jesus stated that loving your neighbor as yourself is second in importance only to loving God. In his Sermon on the Mount, Jesus expressed what has come to be known as the Golden Rule: that in everything, you should do to others as you would expect to be treated yourself.

Generosity in doing good, or "Sadaqah" in Arabic, is a principal virtue encouraged in Islamic ethics and is considered an essential aspect of an observant Muslim's character. Such acts of charity are not just monetary or doing something for someone else, but could simply be a smile or an encouraging word. Going even further, "Sadaqah Jariyah" is a deeper act of kindness, one that resonates in perpetuity in the world after you die.

In ancient African philosophy, *ubuntu* is the idea that my humanity, for example, is bound together with all those around me and with my community at large. As the late Desmond Tutu says in his book *No Future Without Forgiveness*, one who lives in the spirit of ubuntu believes that "my humanity is caught up, is inextricably bound, in yours." This idea is one that stands in vivid contrast, Tutu notes, to the idea that "I think, therefore I am," expressed by the 17th century philosopher René Descartes. Someone who personifies ubuntu is practicing The Generosity Mindset. "A person with ubuntu," Tutu says, "is open and available to others, affirming of others, does not feel threatened that others are able and good . . ."

In the Hindu tradition, the principle of Karma Yoga highlights selfless service, without any anticipation of credit or results. The idea is to let go of attachment to a particular outcome of our service to others, acting from the pure joy of being able to give.

I could cite instances in which a call to generosity is found in other ancient wisdom traditions such as Buddhism, Confucianism, the philosophy of Stoicism in Ancient Greece, and Native American spirituality.

In more contemporary times, the principles of generosity have been expressed repeatedly by businesspeople and business authors. In his book *How to Win Friends and Influence People*, originally published in 1936, Dale Carnegie emphasized that genuine interest in others and focusing on their needs is the key to building influence, developing lasting friendships, and achieving business success.

During his lifetime, noted author and speaker Zig Ziglar repeatedly expressed The Generosity Mindset principle. His most quoted line is arguably, "You can have everything in life you want if you will just help enough other people get what they want."

In his book *Influence: The Psychology of Persuasion*, psychologist and author Dr. Robert Cialdini details the rule of reciprocity. This rule is so fundamental to human behavior, Cialdini notes, that it is baked into our DNA. The rule of reciprocity states that when we receive a gift without strings attached, whether it is a favor, a gift, or an invitation, we have a natural tendency to want to return the favor in some way with a gift of our own. In other words, giving is an essential and inescapable aspect of who we are as human beings.

In their book *The Go-Giver*, authors Bob Burg and John David Mann present a parable that demonstrates what happens through the power of giving and seeking consistently to provide value to others. The story revolves around a young professional who learns that personal and professional success is a natural outgrowth of genuine generosity and service. By serving the needs of others first, this young man finds that unexpected opportunities become available for him.

Adam Grant, an organizational psychologist at The Wharton School of the University of Pennsylvania and bestselling author, has written extensively about giving in business relationships and in the workplace. In his book *Give and Take: Why Helping Others Drives Our Success*, Grant argues that givers—those who selflessly contribute to others without expecting anything in return—can achieve remarkable success in their careers and businesses. He emphasizes that building a culture of generosity and collaboration can lead to long-term benefits and personal satisfaction.

The principles of The Generosity Mindset go back to ancient times and have been expressed and espoused repeatedly ever since. The only problem is that while these principles are easy to celebrate, they are rarely followed consistently. In a "look at me" world wanting instant results, the deep wisdom of The Generosity Mindset is considered too idealistic to be practical and is sometimes overlooked altogether. This is where you, as a professional of value seeking to build your professional services practice, can significantly differentiate yourself and be recognized for who you are and the value you bring.

The Generosity Mindset is a Gift to Clients

Like most solo or small professional services providers, you know that clients come to you carrying what is often a very high level of frustration and angst over a particular problem. Whether it involves their marketing or accounting, a legal issue, or maybe a dysfunctional team, they are burdened with it. Running a small business causes stress on its own, and the weight of the issue that prompted your meeting is piled right on top.

When you as the solutions provider show up with The Generosity Mindset, you recognize and acknowledge the stress that business owner client is experiencing. With such a mindset, you present yourself not as just another vendor, but you elevate your standing in the eyes of clients. You are regarded as a professional of value. That is an enormously generous gift.

Thanks to an increased amount of research in recent years, we know a lot more about how stress and anxiety affect reactions and decision making. Some common findings include:

- Stress and anxiety can lead to reductionist thinking, in which a myriad of possible options is reduced to binary, "all-or-nothing" thinking.
- Stress and anxiety can cause a denial of reality because an individual cannot handle the level of uncertainty they are confronted with in their business and personal lives.
- Chronic stress biases decision making toward habits (the familiar) vs. goals (the unknown).
- Stress and anxiety can cause a person to put off making a decision because they are fearful of making the wrong choice.
- Stress affects the brain's ability to weigh benefits and costs.
- Too much stress and anxiety, experienced regularly, over time, negatively affects health and well-being. At its extreme, stress and anxiety may lead to chronic disease such as strokes or heart attacks.

When you think about what's going on in the head of your client, you come to the table with some compassion, understanding, and yes, generosity. You seek ways to help and solve a problem that your client may not be able to communicate well. When you approach client engagements with The Generosity Mindset—whether an initial value conversation or an emergency cry for help when they think the bottom is falling out beneath them—you offer extraordinary value by slowing down and bringing calm to the situation.

You don't rush in to talk about your service offering. You don't cause anxiety by charging in with sales scripts and memorized counters to objections. You bring two open ears and one mouth to the conversation and use those tools in that proportion. You allow a client to breathe, to unload, and hopefully to get to a point where they share what has been weighing them down. This act alone is liberating for the client.

With The Generosity Mindset, you momentarily readjust the lens of the client, away from the mud of the problems which have you sitting there, and upward to their hopes and dreams for the business and for themselves and their family. You offer a value roadmap which goes well beyond the completion of a set of tasks. You show a client what transformation in their business looks like, and what it does for them personally. You make the cost/benefit considerations easier for that stress-filled client. You quantify the value they will receive. You price to receive a fee commensurate with the client-defined value of the transformation you deliver. Therefore, instead of being viewed by the client as a "sunk cost" or a "necessary evil," you are viewed as an investment.

Establishing The Generosity Mindset

Before you engage with a prospective client, it is vital to prime your Generosity Mindset.

Have you ever been a guest in someone's home, maybe for a holiday party, and asked for the location of the washroom? Has the response included not only the directions, but a "Just don't look in the closet" with a chuckle? What your host is thinking at that moment might be a bit more frantic: "PLEASE, PLEASE, whatever you do, PLEASE don't open that closet door."

Your prospective clients almost invariably have a messy closet, essentially the problems and turmoil underneath, the things the world doesn't see. That's particularly true for do-it-yourselfers coming in from out of the cold. It could be that they've been practicing law without a license (using Google to produce legal agreements), or that their accounting system of choice involves a Nike shoe box.

To be effective in your practice, it is vital to understand where the "closets" of your clients and prospects are located, and to know what those closets contain. As you engage with a prospect, their closets are your competitors—the shoe box accounting system, the free Google documents, or the poorly crafted employee handbook they got online.

Part of your trust equation with that individual involves assuring them that you won't judge them, that no matter how disordered the closet may be, you have seen it so many times that it's not a big deal— at all. As those closet doors start to open and you get the opportunity to peek inside, you must maintain a professional demeanor. You cannot exclaim "Oh my gosh!" You cannot sigh or laugh. The time for laughter will be later, after you've implemented solutions for that client, and in their delight they themselves reminisce and chuckle about how bad things were before you arrived. That's when you can laugh. Further, it is quite likely that prospect became your client without all the closet doors being opened. If that client feels safe to share and isn't worried about judgment, then you'll have the ability to serve them much more effectively—deliver much more value—than you would have otherwise.

Your role, as a services professional, is to allow your clients to breathe, relax, and not worry about judgment. That's a marvelous act of generosity. If you are successful in this regard, you set the stage for a fruitful value conversation and for building trust.

Using The Generosity Mindset to Counter Negative Mindsets

In Chapter 1, I discussed several mindsets which can hold you back as a solopreneur and inhibit the growth of your professional services practice. A mindset is simply a belief, and beliefs can be changed.

By focusing on genuinely serving others and seeing the impact of your actions, The Generosity Mindset offers you a powerful antidote to these negative mindsets. You find that your perspective is reframed from self-centered fears and doubts to a broader, enriching experience of connection and growth with all those whom you encounter.

Let's take each negative mindset we explored in Chapter 1 and discuss how The Generosity Mindset acts to counter each one.

Mindset of Inadequacy

Negative Impact: You don't believe you're good enough or have the necessary experience or knowledge to create a sustainable, thriving business.

The Generosity Mindset Counter: The very act of giving and serving others moves the focus away from the inadequacies you perceive in yourself to the potential you see in others. When you focus on helping others get what they want, and you regularly lift up others, the effect of these small acts accumulates. Instead of questioning whether you are good enough, you witness the positive effects your actions have on others.

Consistently practiced, you receive enough feedback from your acts of generosity to alleviate your feelings of inadequacy. You build confidence in your inherent value as a professional services provider and a human being.

Mindset of an Imposter

Negative Impact: You doubt and discount even your tangible achievements, fearing that somehow you will be exposed as a fraud.

The Generosity Mindset Counter: When you approach others and their problems with the intention to assist in a genuine way, your attention shifts from yourself and your worries about being found out. Your acts of service and the impact of those actions become the focus. Your belief that you are an imposter starts to fade, as your focus is less on proving yourself worthy and more about genuinely serving others. The cumulative effect of your generosity builds self-confidence and dispels your imposter beliefs. As you work to aid others in their journey and see the impact of your actions, you lean into the tangible evidence that you offer genuine value to the world.

Mindset of Comparison

Negative Impact: You continually measure your own capabilities and achievements, and ultimately your worth, to what you perceive in others.

The Generosity Mindset Counter: The Generosity Mindset refocuses your attention away from unhealthy and unwarranted comparisons and toward meaningful connections with others. As you seek to serve first, striving to uplift others and understand their stories, you realize that everyone has a unique journey. You understand that your need to measure yourself against others falls away as you revel in the satisfaction of serving instead.

Mindset of Helping

Negative Impact: Your desire to help everyone is unhealthy. As you spread yourself too thin, you give and do not allow yourself to receive, and you risk burnout.

The Generosity Mindset Counter: A true mindset of generosity incorporates the notion that you and your business must actually thrive in order for your acts of generosity to be sustained. You cannot give water out of an empty well.

Mindset of Scarcity

Negative Impact: You focus entirely on yourself because the world is a jungle with a fixed pie of opportunity. You are fearful and worried about what others will take from you.

The Generosity Mindset Counter: Giving is reciprocal, but not in any quid pro quo way. As you put The Generosity Mindset methods into practice, your actions encourage sharing, collaboration, and generosity in others. Your fear of scarcity naturally diminishes. You also find that your brand image is associated with generosity. Clients and strategic referral partners, overall, prefer to work with businesses that promote mutual growth of each other and in the community at large.

The Irony of The Generosity Mindset

If you keep your focus on the client's needs, hopes, and dreams, you and your practice will benefit by attracting better fit clients at higher fees than you would otherwise garner. You will also have a business you are excited to dive into every day, and you will gain more joy from your work. I'll address this idea in more depth later in the book, but I want to share a brief story now that gives you a sense of what's ahead.

Years ago, I had a conversation with an entrepreneur whose business, while growing, had gnawing problems under the surface, causing her to lose focus and sleep.

"All this is obviously weighing on you," I said. "What would it mean to have these problems resolved?"

She looked up and away, into some place where she could see what her business—and her life—might look like with solutions to the problems she outlined. A wave of relief swept across her face.

"Wow, I'd be a lot less stressed. I wouldn't feel bogged down anymore. I'd have the freedom to make this business a lot larger."

I let that vision linger for a moment, then I asked, "What's that worth to you?"

"Wow," she said, "I can't even imagine."

That wasn't quite true. As our conversation continued, she formulated tangible answers to that question. My value as a solutions provider lay in the answers she herself formulated. That's where my value was rooted, not in what I needed or what I thought I was worth. The concept of "what I'm worth" had nothing to do it.

Bringing The Generosity Mindset to that conversation allowed this harried and frustrated entrepreneur to dream a bit about a less stressful life and what the solutions she craved would allow her to do. In turn, she was able to see that my value to her was much greater than just the business advisory services we were discussing. The value of engaging me was tied up in exactly what she most craved: transformational outcomes for her business which got her out of the rut she was experiencing.

Better pricing for your services starts with a mindset focused on outcomes and solutions rooted in the value clients derive from the work you do. You do not want to be content with getting paid what you think you are worth. You want to crack open the value your clients see and get paid based on a piece of that value.

Defining value based on how a client perceives value is a much more generous way to approach discussing and pricing your services. None of the value focus is on you. It is not about what you think you're worth, and rightly so. It's about the client and where the client sees value. Isn't that a much better crutch to lean on than those self-limiting mindsets we discussed earlier, or pricing like your so-called competition does, or in some vain attempt to define your own value?

Here is the beautiful irony of The Generosity Mindset: The value your clients see in the transformational outcomes you deliver is always more than you see.

To get a better sense of this truth, we need to redefine further what we mean by the term "value."

CHAPTER 3

REDEFINING "VALUE"

Sometimes business owners don't understand the meaning of value. They think value is tied up in the product they sell or the service they deliver, and that it begins and ends there. They think value is what a customer receives when they consume the product or service.

Your service, however, is not "the value," whatever your service happens to be, whether accounting, HR consulting, coaching, exit planning, professional organizing, legal services, or professional speaking. Your value is the resulting transformed business and human being (or a group of them). Your value is what happens as and after that change takes effect for that person or group. So when you talk about what you do, talk about transformation. That is where your value resides. That's what clients happily pay for.

If you are a CPA, tax accountant, or IRS enrolled agent, for example, clients aren't only buying your ability to get a tax return prepared properly. That's

> **"** Price is what you receive. Value, both tangible and intangible, is what the client receives.

assumed. What they yearn for are better results for their business. They are purchasing a less stressful retirement. They are buying the peace of mind of knowing that if they are audited, they will have an experienced professional holding their hand. Yes, a minority of clients are perfectly happy with a tax return being prepared at the lowest possible price. Clients like this do not see any value behind the task itself being successfully completed. They only value the tangible, which in this case is the completion of the tax return.

Most clients, though, are oriented toward not just the tangible, the service itself, but also the value they will receive from the solutions you provide. Different customers have varying notions of what they will pay for that value, but they are value-focused nonetheless.

Your clients buy for intangible reasons, most of which have nothing to do with the features and benefits of the product or service, or what you think might be logical. This principle is true for all customers and everything they buy.

Clients buy solutions to their problems and needs. They buy services which they perceive will enable them to achieve their wants and hopes. They are not concerned about the details that lie between their current-day concerns and the solution they crave. Your service is simply a means to an end, a solution. This truth is an old one, and it will be true as long as people exchange money for products and services. The extent to which you understand and internalize this fundamental aspect of human behavior will drive your ability to define the perceived value your clients place on the outcomes of the services you render. In turn, you will be better able to market to prospects, effectively price your services, and serve the deepest needs of your clients.

Think about it this way: In any transaction in your business, price is what you receive. Value, either tangible or intangible, is what the client receives. Neither of you will agree to that transaction unless you expect to receive a profit. Your profit is the difference between the price you receive and the cost to provide that service. The client's profit is the difference between the value they receive and the price they pay to you.

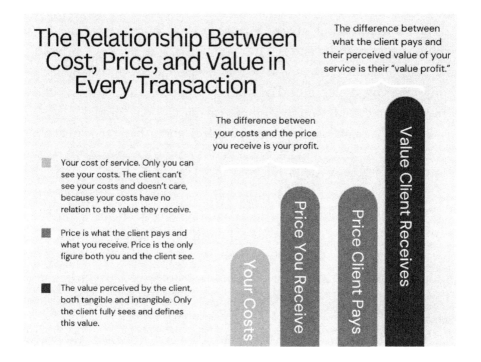

When you focus on the value of the outcomes you generate for clients, you get clearer about how to market your services, whether you should pivot, when to add new service options, and how to price your services, among other business growth decisions. Understanding the value of the solutions you offer clients sheds light on what clients are buying when they come to you.

Because value is intangible, it is defined entirely by the client. Value is not bound by time or space. When or where the transaction happens does not fully define value. Value comes before, during, and after a transaction.

Lessons From A Piano Teacher

I have a friend who, in addition to helping market her husband's business, teaches piano lessons. She has a music degree and is a certified teacher in the Suzuki method of piano instruction. She trained with the founder of the Suzuki method, maintains professional continuing education, and is a top-notch expert in her field. Knowing her personally, I believe her to be kindhearted, easy to work with, and knowledgeable in her craft. Beyond her expertise, she possesses all the qualities you would want in a piano teacher for your child.

During a casual conversation, I asked about her piano teaching. The gentle smile she normally carried on her face disappeared, and her forehead furrowed. She began to speak excitedly and more rapidly.

"Well," she said, "I got fed up with everyone and everything that was going on. I wrote all my clients and fired every one of them."

"Wow!" I said. "Tell me more about that. What was going on?"

"I had parents routinely cancelling or rescheduling at the last minute, mostly because they, their kids, or both were overscheduled. They would ask to come on Sunday, which is a day I try to reserve for family time."

The longer she talked and relived the experience, the more animated she got.

"I had one student whose parent was rescheduling almost every week for some reason or another. The parent was a pain to deal with, always very rude and abrupt." She took a breath and rolled her eyes. She was exasperated by the memory.

"I gave them a list of new stipulations they had to comply with before I would agree to have them continue as my students," she said.

She explained that clients' weekly appointment for lessons was the only time she would see them. She would no longer reschedule appointments, as it caused chaos for her schedule. If they missed an appointment, she explained, they would need to come back at their usual time the following week. She instituted a cancellation policy;

if they cancelled without at least a 24-hour notice, they would still be responsible for payment. She would no longer accept Sunday appointments for any reason.

"Finally," she concluded, "I raised my prices by 35 percent, and I told them that these new terms were non-negotiable!"

"Wow!" I exclaimed. "So what happened?"

At this point, she broke into a broad smile.

"Every one of my clients, except one, accepted my new terms with no pushback," she said. "The only client I lost was the rude parent who I wasn't going to reaccept anyway."

"That's amazing," I told her. "You must have been quite happy about how it all turned out."

"I am, John," she replied. "But what I realized is that my pricing was way too low. After the first of the year, I'm going to raise them again."

By issuing her abrupt ultimatum, my friend unconsciously forced her clients to think about the value she provides versus the new price she was asking. Each client had their own reactions, based on their own individual situation and perceptions of value, as they evaluated whether they would accept this teacher's changes in terms and the new, higher price:

- My child enjoys piano lessons and loves her piano teacher.
- This teacher has already done a superb job with my child, and I expect my child's progress to continue.
- This piano teacher is Suzuki certified. I have no idea where I'll find another Suzuki certified piano instructor.
- I'm not even sure I'll find another piano teacher who my child will like well enough to want to continue their lessons.
- Piano lessons will help my child expand their learning ability and discipline, which might help them get better grades and test scores, ultimately leading to a better college.

- My child may become good enough, with several more years of instruction, to earn a college scholarship.
- Musicians often maintain greater cognitive ability over the long run.
- I like being able to tell my friends that my child plays the piano.
- We'll take a big loss trying to sell the piano we just bought!

Some of these benefits are logical; some of them might make no sense or have any factual basis. Note that some of these considerations, such as selling the piano, have a loose connection, or none at all, to the service and the service provider. Each of these considerations meant more or less than others in the mind of each parent as they evaluated the new, higher price. Whether they sat down and thought this through logically, or whether their consideration was done quickly and informally, all of my friend's clients had one thing in common: they considered the value they received relative to the price being asked. Each client valued my friend's services differently because of their own unique reasons.

What this piano teacher discovered is that all her clients, save the one she wanted to lose anyway, saw more value, both tangible and intangible, in her services than she had seen in them herself when she originally priced her services. The value each of them perceived was still greater than the new, higher price being asked.

The lesson in value that this piano teacher learned is important for you to consider as you evaluate your own business. If you don't clearly understand the value clients perceive—particularly the intangibles—and communicate that value to your clients, both current and prospective, you run the risk of limiting your revenue and business growth, diminishing your profits, and possibly going out of business.

In every transaction, whether it involves piano lessons, business consulting, or even doggie treats, a customer will not buy unless the value they perceive of that service or product is greater than the price they pay. This principle applies to every exchange between customers and producers of products and services. There are no exceptions.

This law is so powerful that it even applies to transactions in which no money changes hands. Think about the sign you see offering "Free Kittens." Of those who drive by without stopping, many are thinking of the long-term cost and commitment of pet ownership. Those costs are greater, in their minds, than the intangible benefits they would receive from a kitten. Otherwise, they might stop.

The price a customer pays goes toward more than a good or service. There are other costs, including your time, experience, or years of study to gain knowledge. Associated costs might also include the equipment you use to perform tasks, subcontractors you hire to support your business, marketing tools, or supplies used. Your clients have no idea of these costs. Actually, they don't care.

Buyers don't have to know the overall costs to acquire a product or service. All they need to possess is a general sense that their perceived value of the product or service exceeds what they have expended to acquire that product or service. If they don't perceive a positive value for the price, they will not buy. If they see enough value beyond the price, they will buy. It's that simple.

The Value Clients See is *Always* Greater Than What You See

Years ago, I was sitting with a potential client who was interested in hiring me to help get his business ready for an anticipated growth spurt. This client proudly talked about the multiple locations he and his wife had opened, how they had grown, cash flow, and how much he was quite certain the business would be valued in a sale. I began to wonder why he needed my advice, since everything seemed so rosy. Then his wife walked into the office.

"Boy, am I glad you're here," she exclaimed. "We have no idea what this business is worth. The books have been a mess since day one. We've got constant turnover, and that means we're working too hard at our age. I want to find a way to get out of this thing. Our retirement is tied up in this business. I need a vacation, and I can't go one more day without us having a plan to figure out exactly what we have here and what we need to do."

The husband sat silently staring at his wife as she went on. She plopped down in a chair and continued: "So I'm glad that he's *finally* called someone to help us sort all this stuff out."

With that truth swirling in the room like a cyclone, the conversation went in an entirely separate direction than the husband originally intended.

This couple represents archetypes of the two distinct mindsets of how clients define their needs and identify value in your work as a professional services provider. The truth-avoiding husband represents the tangible service you provide. That day, it was the analysis of financials, reviewing their processes and hiring approach, evaluating inventory management and marketing, and an assessment of the entire business model.

The wife embodies the intangibles. That meant the worry over having their retirement nest egg tied up in the business, the need for a vacation, the over-working at a time in their lives when they should have been more relaxed, and the stress of turnover and not knowing how to stop the merry-go-round. She was ready to change their lifestyle from one of stress and hard work to one of enjoying their grandkids and taking the trips they had dreamed about.

Your own professional services practice generates these same two sources of value for clients. The tangible is the service you provide, whether it is business advisory work, consulting, legal, accounting and tax planning, or marketing. The tangible is the tactical stuff most services providers sell themselves on: the what and sometimes the how of their offering. The intangibles are what a client hopes they will be able to do, to feel, to realize, and to avoid because of the transformative nature of your work. The intangibles are the value in your work that you might not ever know if you don't

> **❝ Your clients always see more value in your services than you do.**

make it your practice to ask and to understand it from the client's perspective.

Your clients, by definition, see more value in your work than you do, even if they cannot fully express it at first. That's because you cannot know the intangibles they value unless you ask. Therefore, you must ask about and explore the intangibles in a value conversation.

In this dialogue, you ask questions that reveal the hopes, dreams, and fears they have for their business and for themselves and those close to them. Some of these questions, for the client, may not seem germane to your services. Here, you communicate the intangibles of your service offering that clearly address the pitfalls, sleepless nights, and stressful days you help clients avoid. You also describe the transformation you help create for the client: the pleasant experience, the ease of going from where they are to where they want to be, the clarity of knowing what to do next, and a vision of the beautiful end result.

Then you allow the client to express their value perspective. Sometimes they need some gentle nudging. This is where you ask catalytic questions like:

- What do you hope to achieve in your business because of this project?
- How will that change affect you personally?
- What made you decide to do this now?
- Why not do it yourself?

- Out of all the providers you could have called, why did you call me?

For more questions that guide your clients to share their perceived value of their desired outcomes and your services, visit www.thegenerositymindset.com/bookresources.

The answers to questions like these help uncover how a client defines value in the transformational work you do. In the absence of asking such questions, listening to the answers, and following up for further inquiry, you possess little to no knowledge of how the client perceives and defines value in the outcomes you deliver.

Prior to this anxious wife walking in the room, quite willing to discuss the intangible value they were seeking, my focus was on the tangibles: the arc of the business, how it had grown, the financials, and so forth. All that information is vital, of course, but incomplete. If I had listened only to the husband, I would have priced my work based on an incomplete assessment of value. Eventually, through an in-depth value conversation, I would have identified the intangible value they attributed to the services I provide. Thanks to the wife's unprovoked honesty, we arrived at the intangibles quickly.

In this instance, I lucked out. You should never count on luck or uninformed guesses, for that matter. Ask the questions necessary to get to the intangibles. This is where your clients and prospects will find their greatest value in the services you provide. They already assume you know the what and the how of the work you do. Open the door to present them with what they really want—the outcomes you can deliver for both the business and for the business owner personally.

The Value Equation

The value equation states that a buyer will not make a purchase unless the value, which they alone define, is more than the price. Such value can be tangible, like a completed tax return. It can also be intangible, such as the peace and quiet a parent receives after giving their screaming child a taste of your delicious homemade chocolate candy.

The value equation drives all transactions in our economy. Your services are not exempt from this equation. Every transaction, whether it involves a can of green beans, an iPhone, or lawn care service, is subject to the customer's value equation. If you are a professional services provider, it applies to you, too, whether you are a consultant, attorney, CPA, or coach. The value equation even applies to exchanges between two parties which don't involve currency.

THE CLIENT'S VALUE EQUATION

Client Perceived Benefits

Minus

Price

Equals

Value Client Receives

The Current War is a movie that tells the story of the race between Thomas Edison and George Westinghouse to sell their competing visions of an electrical grid in the late 1800s. Edison pushed his original vision of direct current, while Westinghouse championed alternating current. Westinghouse's vision won, as alternating current was less costly and much more effective distributed over long distances.

At one point in the movie, Westinghouse says, "The value of something isn't what someone's willing to pay, but the value of something is what it contributes."

This statement is the value equation at work.

When a client assesses your services, they are judging the contribution your services will make to their business and their life. The only person who can determine this value is the client. It is their perception, their determination, of that contribution.

Westinghouse used the value equation to his advantage. After Edison reneged on paying the talented inventor Nikola Tesla a promised $50,000, Tesla quit and Westinghouse pounced, offering Tesla a royalty of $2.50 per AC horsepower, which would amount to much more than a flat $50,000. Tesla accepted, and Westinghouse's vision was on its way to realization.

The actual history is a bit more complicated, but the movie illustrates the point quite well. All Edison sees is that $50,000 is an immense amount of money. His ego keeps him from seeing Tesla's long-term value to his company. Westinghouse, on the other hand, sees that the ultimate contribution Tesla can make to his company dwarfs even a royalty payment like the one he proposes. The value at stake is immense: the opportunity to build the electrical grid for the entire United States. That is the value equation at work, Westinghouse and Hollywood-style. It is utilized by the buyer in every transaction.

Value and The Generosity Mindset go hand-in-hand. How you, as a services provider, define value is a major determinant of success in your business. If you are focused only on yourself, your service, and what you think you are worth, you will ignore a fundamental law of how your prospective clients gauge value. If, however, you approach clients with The Generosity Mindset, which focuses first on them and how they define value, you will have the necessary foundation for success in your business.

CHAPTER 4

POSITIONING

Positioning is what you say about your business to communicate the kind of clients you serve and how you transform them. It incorporates everything you say about yourself and your firm in brochures or on your website.

Positioning incorporates who you are writing your blog articles or social media posts for. It is what you say about yourself in an elevator pitch and what's on a business card. Positioning is how you market, advertise, brand, and in any way communicate to the rest of the world about who you serve.

Very few of us, when we start out, have the advantage of a ready-made client base. Some consultants might come out of corporate knowing that their first client will be their former employer. Maybe you've left a larger accounting or law firm and several clients, preferring to work with you, have followed you to your new practice.

Many services entrepreneurs, however, don't begin their business with such a head start. Even if they do, some find out that the initial burst of clients who came in the door when it was first opened takes them only so far. You must attract clients to survive and to grow. That is where positioning comes in.

Here's the problem with positioning when you start out, and even when you have been in business a few years and are trying to get to whatever next level you've identified as a goal: You allow your fear and anxiety to determine your positioning.

Once, I was on the phone with a consultant ready to launch his solo practice.

"Who do you serve?" I asked him.

"Businesses between $5 million and $50 million in sales," he replied.

"That's not a niche," I told him. "That's an ocean."

Later, out of curiosity, I looked it up. According to The North American Industry Classification System (NAICS), there are more than three-hundred thousand businesses in the U.S. with sales between $5 million and $50 million. Yes, this consultant is like a dingy in an ocean, and given his expertise, he does not need many clients to have a thriving and lucrative consulting practice. This kind of broad positioning is a common fallacy when starting in professional services, and I understand what's behind this guy's thinking. You're afraid to be specific with who you help because you might exclude yourself from potential new business opportunities. This is a scarcity mindset in action.

Positioning yourself to serve everyone, if you're honest, is selfish. There is no possible way that this consultant, no matter how brilliant he might be, would be the right fit for every one of those three-hundred thousand businesses. Each one involves a unique set of problems. Each one of them has an owner or owners who have their own personality, management style, and background. Yet this consultant was essentially claiming he was the right fit for every one of those businesses.

To be fair, he did not make that claim. If I had been rude enough to ask him why he thought he was qualified to serve such a widely diverse set of businesses, I would like to think he would have told me he wasn't.

The problem with such an overly broad positioning is that it comes across as needy. He came across as a brand-new consultant who needed business to get things going instead of a seasoned professional who just happened to be starting up a new business. He seemed more desperate to get revenue than patient to get the best-fit clients.

Positioning yourself to serve everyone, moreover, makes you the expert at nothing in particular. It's like a coffee shop that serves lukewarm coffee so they will appeal to both the hot and cold coffee drinkers. By positioning yourself too broadly, you appeal to no one.

I once attended a gathering of business owners in which everyone introduced themselves and their business.

A travel agency owner introduced himself and casually added, "Anyone who needs to travel is a good fit for me."

A woman pitching her line of skin care products said, "A good client for me is anyone who has skin."

These pitches are cute, but they are wrong. Wrong for both the business and the client.

If I'm a customer planning a trip, I could be planning a road trip to Charlotte to celebrate Mom's 90th birthday, a hiking trip to Nepal with my son, a strategic planning retreat for my key employees, a cruise to the Mediterranean with my wife, a family reunion in Texas, or a business trip to New York for which I need a conference room. All these needs require different levels of knowledge and expertise.

How many of these various trips has our travel agent qualified himself for? Zero. I have no idea what he's really good at, such that if I'm planning a trip to a destination for which he's the expert, I'd better call him. Further, if he wants me to refer him, I don't know what I can tell anyone about him. He's not memorable. He's a commodity.

Here's the real problem from the customer's standpoint: The person making the appeal sounds like they don't really know what they're doing, or they don't really care about the person they're selling to. They come across as badly needing to make a sale, therefore, they will sell to anyone.

From the travel agent's point of view, broad general appeals can open the door for clients who are not a good fit or who do not want to pay for the work they'll put into planning a trip. Suppose, instead, this travel agent had said, "I'm an expert at planning destination family reunions" or "I just got back from a cruise in the Mediterranean, and one overlooked destination there I highly recommend is Montenegro."

Now, as a customer, I have something to remember him by. If I'm planning a cruise to Europe, I'd better call this guy because he's signaled his expertise. His expertise translates into additional value for customers, and that value for customers helps justify a better price for him. Circumstances like this confirm the truth underlining the cliché that "There are riches in niches." Even if I'm thinking about a cruise to Alaska, this travel professional is much more likely to be qualified to help because he has indicated that he loves to cruise.

Let's say the skin-care lady said that her product restores the needed skin oils lost if you like scorchingly hot showers or baths. If I know how much my wife loves her blistering soaks in the tub, then suddenly the skin care lady has got me thinking. She has positioned herself as a skin care expert. I've not only got a mental hook to remember her by, but I may even be thinking about a gift for my wife—a thoughtful one she's not expecting from a knucklehead husband like me who's normally not tuned into these details. Now I'm thinking I'm willing to pay a premium for such a gift because I am not just paying for the product which my wife will benefit from, but for the reaction I'll get from her when she realizes I've put some thought into this gift.

The positioning pitches that apply to everyone, in fact, apply to no one. That is a terrible place to be when you're trying to attract good-fit clients, the ones who are willing to pay for your expertise.

Your Certifications are Worthless

You are a highly educated professional. Your education includes some combination of an undergraduate degree, graduate school and a postgraduate degree, or a professional designation such as a certified public accountant. Maybe you have achieved certification in a highly specialized subject area. Maybe you can illustrate all the expertise you've acquired through journal articles, industry publications you've written for, or even a book you've authored.

It's not that your certifications are worthless, per se. You worked hard to achieve expertise in your field, and you should be proud of that. In the mind of clients, though, your certifications are just the table stakes. Most clients assume you have the qualifying degrees and training necessary to execute the project at hand.

Many professional services providers, however, believe that their positioning starts with their certifications and continues with the work they do for clients. That is not where successful positioning is grounded at all.

I once had a soloist bookkeeper as a client who wanted to sharpen his proposals and achieve better pricing for his work. I asked him to role play with me as if I were the client and he was talking with me about what he could do for me.

"Well, I'm a QuickBooks Pro Advisor," he began.

"Stop," I said.

"Why?" He had a puzzled look.

"That does nothing for me," I said. I went on to explain to him that there are fifty-thousand QuickBooks Pro Advisors in the United States. He did not make himself unique by telling me that.

I went back to my client role. "Here I am, my books are an absolute mess, and my wife is upset with me that I've missed the tax deadline. I'm bone tired, and on top of that, one of my best employees just quit today. With all that going on in my life, you are sitting here boring me with something I already know. Can you just tell me how you're going to fix my problem?"

I recently had a similar conversation with a leadership coach.

"I'm a John Maxwell Certified Leadership Coach," he said.

"Who is John Maxwell? Is he the coffee guy?"

In both cases, I was role-playing the narrative that is going on inside the head of the clients. Remember from our discussion on value in the previous chapter: Value is defined by what clients perceive. In both cases, these professionals are positioning themselves not from client-perceived value but from their own perspective—their qualifications. Not only is this perspective unhelpful to clients, but it is also counterproductive for the services provider as well.

What if the bookkeeper's opening line, instead of the business about being a QuickBooks Pro Advisor, was, "I pick up after entrepreneurs too busy to do it themselves." The bookkeeper is now speaking this client's language. The client is thinking about how a shoebox full of receipts will get turned into a profit and loss statement which will tell them what they owe in taxes so they can pay on time. They are worried about how they'll be able to deal with that problem and at the same time go through all the pain of replacing that key employee when talent is so hard to find. In one statement, this bookkeeper's perceived value in the mind of this client has soared. This client has been invited to relax and not worry about the shame they feel because their books are a mess. They see a professional of value who can address some of the pressing concerns they have.

What if the leadership coach began a conversation about his work this way: "I make every client I work with a better leader who creates improved performance of their team." Instead of leaning on a reference to a person (John Maxwell) who a client may not know, this coach has reframed his work from the perspective of the client. Frankly, although I know who John Maxwell is, I have no clue myself what I'm supposed to glean about a leadership coach who tells me this other than that they have paid good money to get certified in the John Maxwell program.

Many small business owners know they need to develop their leadership skills so they can attract and retain the employees they need to grow. They do not see themselves, however, as an effective leader. Some think they need to be "charismatic" or some other trait they don't see in themselves. By positioning himself from the perspective of the client, this coach reveals himself to possess a deep understanding of client concerns.

Professionals who illustrate that they have an intimate knowledge of their clients are not only assumed to have the education and certifications necessary to execute transformative work successfully, but they are awarded a much higher perceived value by clients.

Clients are drawn to you when your positioning speaks from their perspective. Those positioning opportunities may be on your website, your LinkedIn posts, or how you talk to clients when they inquire about your services. If this is where you start a conversation with a client, you are starting a value conversation, and that value conversation eventually leads to a much better price, and a client more willing to pay that price than you would have had before.

The Fallacies of Personal Branding

If you Google the term "personal branding" and review the various definitions you find, you will get something like this: Personal branding is how you want people to see you and what you do to shape their perceptions. That definition applies to you if you're a corporate employee, a solopreneur, or a business owner of any size company.

As a solopreneur, you are the creator and deliverer of the service. You are the brand. You cannot hide behind an inanimate product that exists apart from you. Because you are solely responsible for the service and its quality, you are the product. That is why personal branding is so vital to the success of your business, and you neglect it at your peril.

The term "personal branding" can lead you to the conclusion that personal branding is all about you. Just as with education, certifications, and experience, a successful personal branding strategy does not start with you per se. This is why you need to be quite careful before you hire someone to help you develop your personal brand. As the ranks of professional services solopreneurs has continued to expand in recent years, an entire subsector of personal branding solopreneurs has sprung up and grown as well.

Some of them legitimately have advice of value to offer. Some, however, are as bogus as carnival barkers. How can you tell the difference? Be careful when someone comes at you wanting to help you find your "authentic self" or some other navel-gazing phrase like that. Look at their own positioning and see whether they are speaking from the perspective of your problems and concerns as a professional services provider. Test to see whether they have some understanding of your discipline and the unique dynamics of your business. (Remember, you are the potential client here.)

Here is another vital aspect of personal branding you must remember: Your personal brand is what others think or say about you when you aren't around to hear. In other words, personal branding incorporates your reputation. Therefore, you do not ultimately control your personal brand.

Short of hiring someone to help you, what can you do to build an effective personal brand? The first and most essential aspect of a successful personal brand is to DO GREAT WORK FOR CLIENTS. I cannot emphasize this point strongly enough. You can have the loveliest headshot ever taken, the most compelling LinkedIn profile ever posted, the most beautiful website ever conceived, social media feeds which jump off the screen, or any other images of yourself and your practice that you have cultivated and probably paid very good money for. None of that will compensate for poorly done work.

If, however, your clients love you and the transformative work you do for them, nothing is more effective in fertilizing growth in your business. That work will be celebrated by your clients; they will spread the word on what a terrific professional you are; they will gladly write glowing testimonials if asked, and in general will do whatever they can to help you.

Even if you are just starting out, you have pivoted in some way, or for some other reason you don't have a positive personal brand which comes from a reputation for excellent work, there are other ways to build your personal brand. I'll offer some specific ideas in Chapter 11 on relationships and Chapter 12 on marketing and business development. Those suggestions encompass one idea: With everyone you meet, strive to serve. Seek to help others in their journey to get a little closer to their goals. Celebrate them and their work. Operate from The Generosity Mindset. Become known as a professional of value.

In the Dale Carnegie book *How to Win Friends and Influence People in the Digital Age*, the author writes: "The two highest levels of influence are achieved when (1) people follow you because of what you've done for them, and (2) people follow you because of who you are. In other words, the highest levels of influence are reached when *generosity* and *trustworthiness* surround your behavior. [Emphasis mine]"

Here's what's great about The Generosity Mindset and positioning: If you develop and consistently practice generosity, your trustworthiness will skyrocket. Building a personal brand of generosity, if you are sincerely seeking to serve others, isn't either difficult or expensive. When you are known for generosity and trustworthiness, the value of your personal brand will naturally soar.

Positioning with The Generosity Mindset

When you operate from The Generosity Mindset, you surrender the idea that you can serve every client who comes your way. Here's the irony of that generosity: You define your expertise so specifically that it becomes a client attractor. When people know what you do, the intangibles you solve for, and specifically who you transform, you become a magnet for the exact, perfect clients who want to work with you and who value the services you provide.

Years ago, I lived in Memphis, Tennessee. As Memphis is known for its barbeque, entertaining visitors to the city invariably involved a trip to one of the city's well-known spots. Often, that spot was The Rendezvous, the temple of Memphis-style dry-rubbed ribs. While there with several out-of-town visitors, it came time to order. One of my guests, looking up and down the menu, asked the waiter, "What kind of salads do you have?"

The waiter tilted his head down, peering over his glasses and answered, "Man, you're in the wrooooong place."

He wasn't rude. He was making the point that there was a line outside and hundreds of FedEx packages going out every week. (Type "hogs fly" in your browser and see what you get.)

An even more limiting menu, for a long time, could be found at Dreamland BBQ in Tuscaloosa, Alabama. There were only two items on the menu: ribs and white bread. (Three, if you count the sauce you got to dip the white bread into.) At a certain point, they must have lost patience with the questions, because they finally posted a sign: "We serve ribs. We don't serve cole slaw. We don't serve potato salad. We serve ribs." The limited menu didn't hurt Dreamland, either. Without fail, every time I went there, there was a wait.

These two barbecue establishments are iconic because they built a reputation on one menu item: pork ribs. Both have other items on the menu now (yes, even Dreamland), but their renown comes because of one item. That's it.

It's no different in professional services if you want to be recognized as the expert you are. To get there, though, you do not need to go broad, trying to claim expertise in a lot of different areas or serving "everyone." Instead, go deep by defining your specific and unique areas of authority and clearly knowing your narrow target market.

This approach seems counterintuitive, but knowing who you are and who you are not is the kind of positioning you want because it comes from a place of generosity. You are focusing only on the clients who are the best fit for you, who have the greatest need for your services, and who have the highest perceived value for what you do. At the same time, you are honestly communicating to the rest of the world that there are a lot of clients who simply are not a great fit for you, and they shouldn't even bother calling you. That saves them (and you) an immeasurable amount of time and frustration.

What Happens When Your Clients and Network Name You

A former client of mine is the managing partner of a dental-centric law practice with clients in more than thirty states. He is a nationally requested speaker for dental conferences, and he has published numerous articles on dental practice issues in the U.S. and Canada. More important than what I say about him, what his website says, or even what he says about himself, is what his clients say. Once I heard one of his dental practice clients call him "The Godfather." It makes me laugh every time I think about it. Among dentists, that's his nickname.

In one pithy client-bestowed designation, you learn volumes about this attorney. You know this professional holds significant influence within the dental industry and is deeply respected for his insights and experience. Like the Godfather in the famous movie of the same name, this moniker indicates that this attorney is known as someone who possesses the ability to resolve difficult situations.

If you're a dentist, you learn from your fellow dental practice owners that if you have a serious legal problem which might involve a malpractice claim or embezzlement, or you want to sell your practice, you call The Godfather. Maybe you can get away with dealing with your hometown business attorney for the easy stuff, but if your problem is complex or you want to go straight to the authority on a legal matter, you call The Godfather. If you want the enviable position of having your raving fan clients name you, then you cannot be The Godfather of dental law, construction law, manufacturing law, or maritime law all at the same time.

Gregg Burkhalter is an authority on LinkedIn and on using LinkedIn to build a personal brand. While he has forgotten more than I will ever know about LinkedIn, I may know more about Instagram and Facebook than he does (and that's not much, by the way). Gregg had the courage to focus his expertise on the LinkedIn platform.

Even with that specialization, "I'm not the 'everything' LinkedIn expert," Gregg once told me. "I don't do LinkedIn sales training or how to go viral in fifteen minutes on LinkedIn. When someone wants LinkedIn sales training, I refer them to others. My focus is on thought leadership growth and brand building on LinkedIn, which leads to expanding one's professional network and fostering long-term career success."

Gregg notes that the key to positioning is not just specialization, but consistency. "I don't sell," he told me. "I just keep presenting. Over the first eight years of my business, I spoke over 450 times and spread the word on the value of LinkedIn. I didn't try to grow viral. My goal was to build a reputation of value to others."

Like The Godfather, Gregg's clients and his larger network have rewarded him with a moniker he didn't make up himself: "The LinkedIn Guy."

I asked Gregg how his positioning and the moniker which sprung from it has impacted his ability to attract clients and to price his services effectively.

"There's no question that being known as 'The LinkedIn Guy' attracts clients who are predisposed to want to hire me, and to do so at better pricing than I would otherwise be able to maintain."

Generosity Positioning and the Competition

Solo and small firm professional services providers spend way too much time worried about competition. The irony here is rich if you're ex-corporate because your former employer obsessed over competition, market share, and what they would have to report to shareholders next quarter. Leaving big corporate ought to mean you left all that behind.

As a solo or small firm practitioner, you do not have to worry about market share or even the competition. Take the consultant mentioned at the beginning of this chapter. As a solopreneur, he needs only a micro percentage of those 300,000 businesses he identified as his "niche" to do quite well.

As Gregg Burkhalter observed in speaking about LinkedIn, personal branding, and the services he offers, he does not need to work with every prospect who contacts him. He doesn't even need to work with a majority of them. He is able to pick and choose among those prospects he considers a best fit for him and his practice. Those are the clients who see sizable value in the outcomes he delivers and are willing to pay prices which reflect that value.

When you focus on delivering tremendous value to a narrow niche in which you have established your authority, competition becomes an old acquaintance whose face you recognize but whose name you can't remember. Additionally, where value and a well-defined niche converge, your image of the competition changes drastically and you find that it isn't who you think it is.

Hint: Your competition is far from being other service providers in your industry, whether that is consultants, coaches, accountants, or attorneys. Understanding this will help make your positioning much more generous. With a true Generosity Mindset and a clear understanding of your clients' values, you can identify the hidden competitive threats to your practice. Here are a few examples:

- For the owner of a sandwich franchise like Subway, the competition is a convenience store.

- A business attorney client of mine once told me that his competition is the inertia of his small business clients—the reluctance to take the time and spend a little bit to fix a problem agreement.

- For the social media marketing professional, the competition is the client who thinks having a personal Facebook account makes them a social media expert.

- The owner of a jewelry store once told me his biggest competition is Apple Computer. His rationale? That the decision to buy a nice piece of jewelry may get deferred because of a shiny new Mac which beckons.

- For the financial advisor counseling his client to buy disability insurance, his competition is the client thinking, "It won't happen to me."

- For a small business bookkeeper, the competition is an Excel spreadsheet and a shoebox.

Recognizing your hidden competitors helps you understand where your customer sees value—or lack of it—in your offering to them. It also helps with your positioning and the messages you share in your marketing, what you say in your sales conversations, and how you introduce yourself in networking environments.

Speaking of small business accounting and shoeboxes, there is a business tax preparation company in Atlanta called Shoebox Tax Prep. The best-fit clients of this firm recognize themselves in the name—the harried small business owner who doesn't have regular bookkeeping and preparation of financials. When tax time comes, they may be a little insecure and ashamed of that messy box of receipts they've stuffed everything into during the year. They may have even been told by their existing tax preparer that they need to find a new provider because of that mess. While Shoebox Tax Prep could handle the returns for business owners with more organized records, their generosity positioning helps their ideal clients identify themselves. Clients know they will be able to walk in with their shoebox and they will be in a welcoming place to do that.

The irony of employing generosity positioning often means you forgo other business opportunities that come your way. With true generosity positioning, you hold firm to your true client base, forsaking most, if not all others, and you end up attracting clients who are outside your niche. How does this happen? Well, for one, you become the flame that attracts the moth seeking light. Like a magnet, you emit an undeniable frequency of expertise that others cannot seem to ignore. Often, they will come to you as referrals because satisfied clients—the ones who truly value your services—like to talk about and recommend their service providers.

When this happens, you have the option to accept the new clients or provide them with resources and recommendations that are better suited to their values. That puts you in the driver's seat and keeps a steady stream of business flowing your way.

CHAPTER 5

THE VALUE CONVERSATION

Conversations with prospective clients should not be viewed as sales calls. These conversations shouldn't even start with a sale in mind. A better way to frame these conversations is to start with something like, "Let's see if we're a good fit, and to do that, I need to ask some questions."

Then ask those questions. "Why do you think you need X and Y?" "What outcomes are you trying to achieve?" "Why haven't you tried <fill in the blank>?" And so forth. I'll get into more detail below.

A value conversation is a dialogue with a client in which you develop an understanding of how a client defines the value of the outcomes, both tangible and intangible, which will occur because of your work for them.

You are a professional services provider. You serve. Your mission should be to help others find solutions to their problems. When you make that your focus, you will be seen as a professional of value, and, in turn, you will stand out from the crowd.

Instead of thinking of prospect meetings as sales calls, try thinking of them as best-fit conversations, value conversations, or even just a regular conversation. Do whatever is necessary to put yourself in The Generosity Mindset as you prepare for these conversations. A piece of that mindset is having the patience to understand the client who is sitting in front of you. If you don't understand the motivations driving that client, then you won't be adequately serving that client, and your pricing will be wrong. You won't be serving the interests of either of you.

Here is another way to think about it. As a solopreneur, the word "sales" may give you sweaty palms and shortness of breath. It might be the one facet about your business you hate or fear (or both) the most, besides networking. There are several reasons for this, including:

- You may be resentful because when you started your business, you thought your technical skills, experience, or degrees and certifications were all that mattered. You've learned they aren't.
- You think sales is only for extroverts, and you're an introvert.
- You think sales means doing an impression of the loudmouth guy on late night infomercials selling aluminum siding.

The solution to your issues around the sales call (a term that I hate) is a mindset shift: You're just having a conversation. The person you are visiting with has a problem, thinks you can help them, and you are trying to do just that. That help may or may not involve your services. Quite often it will, but that's not the mindset with which you conduct your conversation. You're just going to chat with a new friend.

A low-key conversation causes trust to grow and allows you to learn more about that business owner than you would otherwise. You get a better sense of what they need, whether they are a fit for your practice, and if you get to the proposal stage, you can price your services more effectively.

Moreover, if you are an introvert or lean that way, the value conversation is made for you. I find that introverts are often much better at conducting effective value conversations than extroverts who are supposedly better at sales. Embrace your introvert qualities. By doing so, you are much more likely to stay calm and patient, and build trust while doing so, instead of talking too much. You'll be better at listening to understand as opposed to thinking about what to say next. By definition, you're not high pressure. Lean into all this.

In his book *The Secret of Selling Anything*, Harry Browne writes: "Everyone is already motivated. The only question is 'By what?' Your job is to find out what it is that motivates your prospect. . . . Don't confuse products with motivations. No one ever buys a product. He buys what the product will accomplish. He buys because there's something he wants for his life. Your job is to find out what that something is."

Prior to the value conversation, you prepare by getting into The Generosity Mindset like we discussed in Chapter 2. You offer yourself as a guide who will generously help them on their journey as a possible buyer, offering pointers on issues they need to think about as they make a decision. You map a solution for them. That solution might not include working with you, but you generously offer resources, advice, or insights to help the prospect get closer to obtaining the value and solution they seek.

If you come to this dialogue genuinely seeking to serve first, regardless of whether that service results in a sale for you, you will reduce the tension and anxiety that person feels about having made the call to you in the first place. You also relieve yourself of the pressure to say all the magic words to convince the prospect to become a customer. Finally, you end up with a better engagement, should you make the sale, and at better pricing than you would have otherwise. (More on that later.)

A successful value conversation has three essential components:

1. Set Client Expectations: Set the stage with the prospect for the upcoming value conversation.

2. Widen a Client's Perspective: In the value conversation itself, widening a client's field of vision to see more fully how value will be generated by the project at hand.

3. Establish Client Perceived Value: Together in that dialogue, establish and define the value the client sees in the outcomes.

Set Client Expectations

There are two vital expectations you should create as you engage with a prospect: 1) that you genuinely care about their needs first over yours; and 2) that you are focused on delivering value to them that they will help define.

You should clearly state, on the front end, that you may or may not represent the solution to their problems and issues. Even if you are 100 percent convinced that you are the right provider for them, you don't know that for sure until you have a full value conversation. Therefore, offer a statement such as, "We need to have a conversation to see whether I can help you solve your problem. If I can't, then I'll help you find someone else who can."

When you genuinely offer yourself as someone who can map out a solution—and believe that yourself—instead of being an unctuous salesperson simply trying to ring the cash register, you build trust with that business owner.

The other expectation you want to establish, if the two of you determine that you are a great fit, is that the framework of the economic relationship you will have will be grounded in the value of the outcomes you help them achieve. You must clearly state that you are all about delivering value, and that value will be significantly greater than the price they will pay to receive it.

Here's one suggestion:

"Ms. Client, a business relationship between the two of us will only work if I deliver tremendous value for you. Let's agree that we'll only work together if the value of the solutions I offer you significantly exceeds the fees you pay to me in return."

You are a solutions professional bringing value to this relationship. You must get your client to think of an engagement with you as an investment in which they will receive a significant return of value to them and their business. By doing this, you will have elevated your value by reframing a transaction the client might have viewed as a commodity into an investment in a trusted advisor. This reframing will come back to benefit you later when the conversation turns toward pricing.

Widening a Client's Perspective

In the value conversation itself, your goal is to create an environment that allows the client to fully express their hopes, dreams, fears, and concerns. You want to get beyond the need that has prompted the conversation to begin with.

For example, if you are a CPA, a client may have contacted or been referred to you because they need better tax return preparation and advice for their business than they currently have. That is the task the client sees you as the professional performing for them. The outcome they are looking for, however, goes much deeper. Getting a better tax professional in place could be one piece of a much bigger puzzle, such as preparing the company for an important stage of growth or for an exit from the business altogether.

Many clients are good at recognizing symptoms, but often they do not understand root causes. If you don't cure root causes, the symptoms will linger. Moreover, every client is different. Your leadership training modules, for example, may have worked wonders for the referring client, but that is not what the prospect in front of you needs.

Further, clients do not understand everything you do. They don't know about the technological changes in your industry which have allowed you to add insightful analytics. They don't understand how your practice has evolved to a more comprehensive service offering.

Let's take the example of the professional organizer. If the client has a problem in the garage and the home office, it's not just a matter of coming in and cleaning up the mess in both places and moving on. If that's all you do, you are experienced enough to know that in a matter of weeks those two places in the home will be right back in the same condition in which you found them.

You've been around long enough to know that a client may have an emotional attachment to objects in both places, which is revealing and should be addressed, if they will allow it. The fact that a client has a neat home otherwise, but has difficulty staying organized in those two isolated places, might reveal some mindset issues which you could help them with, mindsets which, once changed, can lead to a long-term cure.

You might find that the client has a system within the mess that's valuable. Your role will be to help them distinguish between which of their past habits are worth keeping and accentuating and which of those habits need to be discarded along with what's going to the trash heap. Such work requires more than sending in the clean-up crew. It requires a deeper dive with that client that goes beyond the work itself. Your service offering may include the continuing involvement necessary to coach them to modifications in mindset and habits that will bring about systemic change. Coaching may be right there on your website, but your referral partner who sent you that client doesn't know that you've added this service offering.

Further, if the home office is a mess, the work office might be just as bad. This client called you because of a particular need at home, but they don't know that you handle workplace settings as well. They know you can organize their garage, but they don't know you are also a master at organizing self-storage spaces.

Because I've worked with enough professional organizers on their pricing, I know that their expertise encompasses a broad range of service offerings. Most clients who are referred to or find a professional organizer online, though, have no clue. All they see is the problem at hand, and that is what they are calling about. It is vital for you as the expert to walk them through the implications of what a successful engagement with you would mean, both short and long term, for them and their business. When you do that, you further establish yourself as the authority they should engage, and you build trust as you do.

Establish Client Perceived Value

You establish the value of the outcomes a client sees in an engagement with you while you are having the value conversation, not after. Once you have completed that conversation, both you and the client should have a grasp of and agreement on value. In addition, the client should see more value in successful outcomes than they did before the conversation, simply because you have widened their perspective to see the intangibles they might not have thought of.

For the CPA mentioned above, it is imperative that she open a client's mind to the idea that the additional value they will derive from a successful cycle of company growth or from an exit is exceptionally larger than the short-term impact of saving on this year's tax bill.

For our professional organizer, he must be able to explain the long-term value of breaking bad habits around organization. Therefore, the client sees that such value is extraordinary relative to the short-term thrill of that fully organized garage and home office.

To do this, you must be curious and excel at asking catalytic questions. Catalytic questions are those queries that cause the person asked to lean back and say, "That's a great question" as they consider the answer. These are the questions they do not take the time to mull over, or only do so when they're far away from their business with time to think. Catalytic questions provoke deeper thinking not only about what clients think they need, but also about the wider business and the goals they have both for the business and for themselves personally.

Systematizing Better Listening

The more skilled you are at listening, the more effective you will be at having a value conversation that diagnoses a client's needs, hopes, dreams, and fears. In turn, you will be better at serving that client and at pricing your services.

Quite simply, there is a direct connection between better question-asking and listening skills to the bottom line of your practice. Studies consistently reveal that all of us overestimate our listening ability. "All of us" includes me. So writing about the subject helps me, and I need all the tutoring and reminders I can get on this subject.

For some, having a system helps break bad habits. We are all at different points in our ability to listen effectively, and you practice and use those better listening tactics that best work for you. Be careful, though, to ensure you are not such a captive of a complicated system of listening tactics and tips that your system not only cancels out its purpose for you, but also becomes painfully obvious to the client.

For example, mirroring what others say is a technique in which you paraphrase what someone has just said in order to show you are engaged in the conversation. A client might say they are concerned about their process around inventory management. Then you, mirroring them, might respond that what you hear them saying is that they are concerned about inventory management. Such a tactic runs the risk of making you sound stilted as opposed to the intended purpose of establishing a rapport and building trust.

Utilizing a value conversation is my own way to systematize better listening. If I remain in an inquisitive mindset, more interested in the other person and their situation than my own, I will be better able to ask vital catalytic questions.

While I'm careful about not creating too many stilted tactics, here is one trick that is easy to remember, courtesy of blogger and podcaster Mike Crittenden: Ask three good questions before you offer your own opinion or statement.

Mike notes that when you follow this rule, you'll achieve two vital outcomes: 1) People will feel heard and will be more encouraged to speak up; and 2) Your opinion, when it comes time to share it, will be better informed. That is exactly what you want in a value conversation.

An effective value conversation with a prospective client obviously involves more than three questions. What Mike is pointing to, though, is having enough of a mental system on which you can rely to break your natural, human tendency to jump in too quickly and open your mouth.

If you are not a great listener or if you are worried about your tendency to jump too quickly to propose solutions, bring a notebook with prepared questions or prompts. You will be better equipped to get the answers needed to either craft the ideal solution or refer them to someone else who is a better fit.

Sample Questions for a Value Conversation

There is no one right way to conduct a value conversation, other than to make sure you ask about and explore the intangibles. That conversation can be held in one sitting, or it can be a dialogue held over several different points in time. A value conversation is just that, a conversation. It is not an interrogation. It is a natural exchange. A great value conversation should be a trust builder, and trust is built as you develop the rapport that comes from a natural dialogue.

I have developed a list of sample questions for you to get ideas of questions you might ask in a value conversation to adapt to your own practice and circumstances. Whatever you do, please do not go right down this specific list. Every professional services discipline has its own dynamics and parameters which necessitate specific questions.

Most important, every client is different, even those who have similar businesses. While there are some questions which are similar in their intent and the response you're looking for, this list is hardly exhaustive. You're talking with another human being, which means every value conversation takes contours which are determined, in part, by the person to whom you are speaking.

Here, you communicate the intangibles of your service offering that clearly address the pitfalls, sleepless nights, and stressful days you help clients avoid. You also describe the transformation you help create for the client, the pleasant experience, the ease of going from where they are to where they want to be, the clarity of knowing what to do next, and a vision of the beautiful end result. Then you allow the client to express their value perspective. Sometimes they need some gentle nudging.

For ease of your consideration, I have grouped these questions into five different categories:

- Understanding Basic Client Needs
- Defining and Prioritizing Value
- Budget and Time Constraints
- Understanding Client Expectations and Commitment
- Exploring Alternatives and Closing Questions

For additional questions in each category that can support your value conversation, visit www.thegenerositymindset.com/bookresources.

Understanding Basic Client Needs

Beyond the basics of why the client contacted you to begin with, you want to get an understanding of pain points quickly. Further, you want the client to articulate and feel that pain as you chat.

Here are some sample questions along with what you hope to learn from the answers:

- **Can you describe your company's current situation and needs?** This goes beyond the project at hand to the bigger picture of where the business sits currently.

- **What is your ideal outcome for this project?** An initial shot at how the client defines value.

- **Who are the key stakeholders in this project?** This question helps determine whether others should be at the table for the discussion you are having.

- **How are you currently addressing this need?** Coupled with the next question, you're starting to help the client define their pain points.

- **What have you tried in the past to solve this problem?** Answers to this question will not only uncover pain points, but also possibly dysfunction around how problem-solving decisions get made.

- **What will happen if this issue isn't addressed soon?** Essentially, you're asking "Why not wait?" You want to understand the pains (and their tangible and intangible costs) which are sharp enough to cause this prospect to make a change.

Defining and Prioritizing Value

Here is the meaty part of the value conversation: getting the client to think in terms of the tangible and intangible value they will receive from the transformation you'll help them achieve. You are helping the client visualize what those outcomes look and feel like, and then to express, as best they can, their perception of the value of those outcomes.

Here are some sample questions for defining and prioritizing value, along with what you hope to learn from the answers:

- **For this project, what does value mean to the organization and to you personally?** *Their* definition of value, which you will help them further develop and define in this conversation.

- **How much time or money could be saved with an effective solution?** A question most clients have given at least some thought to. As it relates to time, you need to have the client express what that "found" time—whether it's more family time, vacation time, time to reinvest in other aspects of the business, and so forth—is worth to them.

- **What are the tangible and intangible benefits you are seeking from this project?** You are ultimately going to help them see more value in the outcomes of the solutions to their problems than they initially dared to consider.

- **What are the critical features or aspects you need in the solutions we're aiming for?** A direct question to uncover client-perceived value.

Budget and Time Constraints

Budget and time constraints represent priorities. Lack of budget or not enough time is not a scarcity problem, but a matter of what issues and concerns the prospective client gives primacy to.

Here are some sample questions along with what you hope to learn from the answers:

- **Do you have a budget allocated for this project?** An important question to get some sense of their spending priorities and an idea of the amount they are willing to invest in an engagement with you.

- **Is there flexibility in the budget if it means a higher value outcome?** Essentially: "Would you spend more if I could show you that you will receive more value than you originally thought possible?"

- **How quickly do you need this solution implemented?**
  Urgency is an important client value. Remember that urgency
  can be created by other parties not in your conversation, like the
  spouse of a business owner or the board of directors.

- **What happens if you do nothing?** Another question that
  will help determine both priorities and urgency.

Understanding Client Expectations and Commitment

Here is a vital set of questions, as clients can often have rosy
expectations about the time it will take before they see the first signs of
positive outcomes from an engagement. Be clear what is required of
them to start seeing those outcomes, as very few professional services
engagements are one-way arrangements. Virtually all engagements
I know of require client involvement and response along the way.
Further, understanding client fears is particularly crucial, as fear is a
powerful motivator to avoid action.

Here are some sample questions along with what you hope to
learn from the answers:

- **What are your biggest concerns about this project?**
  Establish client perceived risks, and therefore, their deepest
  fears.

- **What could potentially prevent this project from
  moving forward?** Same as the previous question.

- **Who will own this project for your team?** Your success
  in working with this client depends on your relationship
  with this key contact. Moreover, this individual must have
  enough authority and ability internally to move the project
  forward.

- **How much time do you have to commit to the project
  when needed?** Very few professional services engagements

occur with zero involvement from the client. You need to gauge their level of commitment to keeping the project moving when their input is needed.

- **How would you like us to communicate with you throughout the project?** Their idea of great communication might be so different from yours that you determine they are a bad fit.

- **What would make you consider this project a success?** There are several ways to ask this question, and you are looking for both tangibles and intangibles.

- **What happens if you do nothing?** Doing nothing means the problem will get worse. You want the client to consider what the risks and costs are of that worsening situation.

Exploring Alternatives and Closing Questions

Several of these questions start cracking open the value clients see in you and your firm versus alternative solutions to their problems. Diving deeper with alternatives will help with your pricing later on.

Here are some sample questions along with what you hope to learn from the answers:

- **What makes a provider like us the best fit to solve the problem?** With this question you are hopefully establishing value in you and the solutions you will craft.

- **Have you considered any alternatives to our services?** What you want the client to express is why addressing the problem by hiring you is better than hiring someone else, doing the work internally, or some other way. It is not only about competitors, but also about alternative ways of fulfilling the objective.

- **What are the next steps from your perspective?** As the expert, you should be the one to provide an answer to this question, but it could be that there are some lingering issues which haven't been addressed yet.

- **What is your contingency plan if the project faces unexpected challenges?** The extent to which a client has no other contingency plans, the higher the perceived value the client will have in the project's outcomes.

An Impatient Garage Door Repairman

One day I woke up, sleepily took care of our morning potty time for our dogs, and as I brought in the last one and lowered the garage door, disaster struck. As the door lowered, it crinkled.

My wife couldn't get out of the garage. Fortunately, I was parked outside and could take her to the school where she teaches. On the drive over, she asked who I was going to call about our problem. "I have no idea," I told her, "but I'll work it all out."

After I dropped Dr. Ray off, I went straight to my desk and started my own work. I could deal with that garage door later. A few hours went by before my wife called me during her lunchtime planning period to check on how that garage door repair was going.

"I'm working on it," I told her.

Dr. Ray has a keen nose for bull. "You need to know that I am not spending the night in that house tonight if that garage door is not fixed."

You might say my priorities had suddenly been realigned. I had to get on the stick and make something happen.

With no contacts among garage door installers, I did what most people do in such circumstances these days: I went online. Searching for a garage door expert with what seemed to be satisfactory and legitimately honest reviews, I found a nearby provider who seemed pretty good, and I gave him a call. I described the problem, gave him my address, and texted him pictures of the door along with measurements of the door panels.

After a few minutes, he called me back. "I've got the panels we need to replace the door," he said. "Are you open for me to come out there this afternoon?"

"Yes," I said, trying to damper my excitement.

"Normally I'd charge $1,100 or so, but if you'll pay cash, I'll charge you $800."

"Get on over here, man. I'm headed to the ATM."

I get a sizeable discount for paying in cash, and I'm not going to be in trouble with Dr. Ray? I felt like I was at the casino and three cherries had just come up on the slot machine. With no idea what a garage door replacement like this should cost, I had visions of four figures dancing in my head before this conversation, so that's what I was braced for.

In his impatience to get the job (and seemingly to avoid taxes by receiving cash), my garage door repairman screwed up. He was focused only on the job at hand, not the why of the job. He didn't have a value conversation with me, his client. He never asked me any questions that would have revealed my sense of urgency.

He could have asked questions such as:

- What happened and when?
- Do you know why it happened? Anything unusual happening prior to the problem?
- What did you have in mind to replace the door?
- Any upcoming outside house painting or remodeling?
- When was the house built?
- Any issues with the garage door motor itself?
- How many cars are parked in the garage?

He could have then said, "My crews are pretty busy right now, and we're more than halfway through the day today. When did you need to have the work completed?"

At some point in this conversation, I would have revealed the big problem, which had little to do with the garage door itself. It was important to my wife that this job be completed that day, and therefore it was important to me. I would have understood that I'm calling him in the middle of the day, hoping that he can get my replacement done by day's end. If he had told me that for a rush charge, he'd get out there that afternoon, I would have paid who knows how much: $1,500? $2,000? I don't know what I would have paid, but I felt like I'd drawn the "Get out of jail free" card to pay only $800.

In the services business—home, professional, or otherwise—the price you ultimately receive is based in part on your willingness to have a value conversation which taps into the hopes, fears, dreams, and other emotions bubbling within your customer. Your impatience can cost you a lot of money, like it did my garage door repairman. You might also be like I imagine he could be, wondering why you're working so hard for so little on the bottom line.

Answering the "How Much Do You Charge?" Question

Sometimes, even before you get to have the value conversation, someone you meet at a networking event or through a referral or even in the grocery store might ask, "So, how much do you charge?"

Respond using The Generosity Mindset.

First, think before you speak. Ask yourself why this person would even ask this question. After all, they haven't expressed their problem or need, and they don't even have a good picture of the services you offer. That means they have no reference point for assigning any value to you or any dollar amount you might share in response to this question.

Once you have taken a breath, simply reply with, "I don't know, we need to have a conversation about your situation and needs and see if we are a good fit . . . I'm not a good fit for everyone."

If the prospect is willing to take you up on a conversation, then you can take the meeting, even if you really don't think they are a fit. Why? You never know until you have a conversation, right? They may surprise you. Also, if they are taking you up on your terms, which is having a conversation about their needs, then you need to fulfill your part. This meeting may be an investment in a future client. It could be an investment in someone who will refer you to another client. It could be that you are just taking a few moments to be kind, to listen, and to offer a few helpful suggestions to a new business owner. That's part of The Generosity Mindset.

It's important to focus on prospects who are willing to discuss their needs up front and in some detail. You will end up with clients whose needs you are meeting and who are a good fit for you. You'll also end up working for a price which is appropriate for the value you provide.

One videographer I know gets it right when it comes to the question, "How much does a video cost?" He frequently has people ask him this question, as if purchasing a professional video for a business is like buying a jar of mustard. His answer to this question is, "We need to have a conversation so I can make sure our talents match your vision."

I love this answer because it introduces two elements which most clients would concede require a conversation. First, there's the need to understand the client's vision for the video. A great business video is like the cliché about beauty: it's in the eye of the beholder. Unless my videographer friend understands what the client sees in their mind when they think about a possible video, he can't even determine what it will take to execute the project, much less submit a proposal.

Second, there's the talent of my friend and his team, which may not be a fit for someone who wants a birthday party video for their five-year-old, for example. Professional talent must mesh with the client vision, and to understand whether that's possible, careful planning is required. That planning begins with a value conversation. It's the first step in establishing win-win client relationships.

Common Issues and Mistakes to Avoid in a Value Conversation

In the pages that follow, I will dissect several common mistakes which pop up as you refine your ability to conduct a successful value conversation, including making faulty assumptions, selling to your own wallet, and appearing too desperate to land the business. I'll also address an extremely common obstacle a client will throw in your way as you attempt a value conversation: trying to get to cost of the engagement prematurely.

Don't fill in the blanks

When engaged in a value conversation with a prospective client, you might sometimes get anxious and impatient. Sometimes the prospect is reticent, or maybe they're busy. They think they already know what they want, and they believe that some of the questions you ask aren't relevant or that you're just making conversation. They react by shutting down or trying to pivot the conversation to your solutions.

Instead of exercising a bit more patience or engaging the client from another direction which might yield the answers you're looking for, you might end the value conversation and move on. That is a mistake.

If you haven't had a deep enough value conversation with a client, you are bound to experience one or several of the following outcomes when crafting options to put in a proposal: 1) You'll make conjectures, some of which may be half right, some of which may be dead wrong; 2) You'll end up proposing solutions which may not fit the needs of the client, and you might lose a good engagement; 3) You might end up with a client who is a bad fit for your practice; or 4) You might end up mispricing the engagement. Avoid all these unwanted outcomes by slowing down and being patient. With this in mind, you always conduct a thorough value conversation.

The stench of desperation

The stench of desperation is the undeniable air of fear you send out when you communicate your 24/7, always ready, no-matter-what availability. Most often, you give off the stench without knowing it. What you might think you're communicating with these messages is your willingness to go the extra mile for clients, but what's really happening is the opposite. They are receiving the message that business is slim, or you are needy, or that you will take whatever project comes your way, or that you are willing to drop an important project, namely theirs, if some other client comes along waving a golden carrot in your face.

Sending such signals, inadvertently or on purpose, indicates that you are too available. Your prospective client might think that the reason it's so easy to get an appointment is because you don't have any clients. It doesn't matter that you have plenty of business, but they just happened to reach out at exactly the right time for an open spot on your calendar. A client might sense neediness that doesn't exist at all.

Another area of availability which signals neediness is when your messaging about your advertised seminar or workshop consistently reminds prospects that there are "just four slots left," and those slots are offered at a discount "so we can wrap up registration." Please don't do this. The marginal revenue you get from one or two more buyers is not enough to compensate for the stench of desperation inflicted on those who might buy your services in the future.

Recognition of availability flows the other way, too. Pay attention to availability, both how you communicate it, and how your prospective clients communicate their understanding of it back to you. Don't think that because clients cannot see your empty dining room, those prospects can't tell what the real deal is. On the contrary, they catch the scent.

What message are you communicating, for instance, when you send emails at 2 a.m.? Even if you are wildly successful and simply enjoy working the vampire shift, a client may interpret a 2 a.m. email as one sent by someone who isn't that successful or experienced and desperately needs the business.

Here are a few ideas to avoid giving off the stench of desperation:

- Bring your servant self, not your needy self. The conversation is not about you and what you need.

- Focus on building a relationship. Be human. Ask the same questions you would ask someone at a party who you're getting to know. Be curious about them beyond just the business itself.

- Listen to understand first; speak second. While it is referred to as a value conversation, this dialogue should be heavily one-sided in favor of the client. They are there to outline their problems, needs, hopes, and dreams. You are there to hear all of that. You cannot hear it if you're thinking about what to say next to counter or to sell something.

- Believe in the value of the outcomes you deliver. You're not a fit for everyone, and not everyone will understand the value of your outcomes. You reduce your perceived value to a client when you press them when they don't have a need or cannot grasp your value.

Allow for space and room to relax and breathe. Business owners today have a heightened sense of smell for high-pressure tactics. They have their guard so high that often they sense sales pitches that aren't even there. Stay calm. The client will pick up on your lack of anxiety, and you will give them the precious gift of being able to breathe and relax themselves.

Selling to your own wallet

While advising a professional services provider on engagement options she was preparing to deliver to a prospect, we discussed the client's needs, wants, and values, the three options that made sense considering what it seemed the client valued, and the pricing of those options.

The pricing of all three of these options was significantly higher than what she had originally envisioned, and well beyond what she'd ever received for any client engagement.

"I'm not sure I would pay that much," she said.

"Who cares what you think?" I replied. "You're not the one writing the check."

This individual was guilty, in that moment, of selling to her own wallet. As it turns out, she hadn't had a deep enough value conversation with the prospect.

When you haven't had an effective value conversation with a client, your conversations have turned more on what the prospect has asked for, your service, and how you do what you do. When it comes time to put together engagement options, you find out that you don't know that prospect as well as you would like because you didn't have the patience to ask friendly yet probing questions that reveal their motivations, values, hopes, and fears. You haven't discovered, for example, that if this guy doesn't complete the project you've been discussing with him very soon, his wife may cause him to end up on a missing persons list. (Remember my experience with the garage door?)

Selling to your own wallet often happens, as was also the case with the garage door repairman, when you are proposing prices much higher than you have ever received for your services. It is the professional services provider's version of the high wire, and the higher the price points, the further off the ground that wire seems.

You're standing on the ledge, about to walk out on the high wire, and your legs are frozen. The wind is kicking up and your stomach is churning. You are deathly afraid of that first step you'll take when you slide the engagement options across the table to the prospect. You're afraid the shock of their reaction to your pricing will blow you right off the wire.

The power of an effective value conversation is that it arms you with confidence. That tightrope feels like it's only a foot off the ground. A fruitful value conversation enables you to keep subsequent discussions around price aligned with the clearly perceived value that you and the client have already diagnosed and discussed. It takes away that queasy feeling in your stomach. It also tamps down the notion that you're gouging someone. When you utilize value pricing, you establish the "value profit"—the excess of value the client receives over the price paid—that the client will receive from your engagement. It's clear, both to the client and in your own mind, that there is a rationale for your price. You feel confident in the value of the work you're doing, and the client profits as well. That's what it's all about.

Price is a story. When you've had an effective value conversation, you can confidently communicate not only value to a prospect without hesitation, but a price to that prospect without fear. You must believe that your solutions are worth what you charge if you expect your prospect to believe it as well.

Value Conversations Help You Avoid Mismatches

If you are not willing to have a conversation with your prospective client about their values, needs, pain, hopes, dreams, and fears, then you might be setting yourself up for a mismatch that could lead to any combination of bad results that include a misunderstanding on scope of services, you leaving money on the table, time wasted on both sides, a relationship that goes sour, or no sale at all.

Poor outcomes occur when you refuse or are too impatient to have a value conversation, and because you don't have several services a client can select from based on what they value.

Having a value conversation and differentiating your services offering is not just about getting the best overall price you can. It's about meeting client needs in a way that creates a mutually satisfying business relationship. When you don't begin the relationship with a value conversation, you run the costly risk of accepting a mismatched client, which can lead to even more problems for you down the road. When you take on a mispriced or an otherwise mismatched project, you eventually grit your teeth and bear it. All the while you think you're hiding your resentment, but you're not. Clients can feel it. Clients know when it's not a good fit, but they've paid you, and they expect you to deliver on your promises.

If, when you sit in front of a prospect, you are already mentally depositing the check you think they might write you, instead of thinking about how you can help them, they know. The prospect can smell the stench of desperation from miles away. This mismatch might not seem like a big deal upon the initial payment, but believe me, it will eventually become a boulder around your neck as time passes.

Clients are just like your spouse or significant other. When your body is physically with them, but your head is a million miles away, thinking about something else, they know. They can see the glazed look on your face. Clients are also like your dog. If you're anxious, your dog feels it, and clients do, too. You have become distracted, over-worked, or otherwise disengaged, all leading to an eventual mismatch.

If you haven't prepared for that meeting, clients know. That client who used to be important to you because they took a chance on you early on in your practice? When they are not treated the same way as they were early on because subconsciously you think you've graduated to larger relationships and you see them as smaller than your more recent clients, they sense it. You may not see it yourself, but they do. You have pulled away from them and are now mismatched.

If you're working for an enterprise client and you're sucking up to the key decision makers while tolerating the junior folks, you may think you can hide that. You can't. Both can sense it. It's a mismatch, and clients know.

You can avoid all of this with a sincere and effective value conversation. Remember that value conversations are not just a method to determine and improve your pricing. The conversation itself can offer a tremendous gift for your clients. Offer it freely and generously, and watch what happens.

Value Conversations Are Acts of Generosity

Great value conversations spring from The Generosity Mindset. You are taking the time to listen to the client and gain a keen understanding of their dreams, hopes, fears, and needs. You are offering yourself as a professional of value, regardless of whether that client ends up hiring you. You genuinely care about serving them and helping them along the journey toward realizing their dreams for their business and personal life.

When you operate from The Generosity Mindset, you are also operating with a mindset that organically rewards you and your business over the long haul. You are seen as a professional of value. You attract clients to you. You become the first choice for colleagues and friends to refer others to. Ultimately, you create more joy in your business.

CHAPTER 6

DIAGNOSE THE CLIENT

The quality of a future business relationship is something every services provider wrestles with. There is no single way to ensure you will always get it exactly right. That said, being strategic in your initial engagements with prospects is crucial to helping you make the right call as to whether you take on a new client. As mentioned earlier, bringing on a new client is not about adding more revenue to your bottom line—it's about being a good fit and being of service.

For every client that's a good fit for you, there are dozens who are not. So how do you identify those who aren't worth your time? Perfecting the value conversation is a great start. There is another, rather unorthodox, method that serves as a simple way to determine whether you should take on a prospective client. I call it "the dinner test."

After your first meeting with the prospective client, and after you've had a meaningful value conversation, take a step back and ask yourself if you would be willing to invite this client to dinner in your home. Not at a restaurant, where it's easy to escape, but to your home. Further, would you be willing to introduce your spouse or significant other to this client? If the answer to these questions is no, then why would you take them on as a client?

Even if you conclude that you would, in fact, be willing to invite the prospective client to dinner at your home, there still might be rough spots in the relationship after you take them on as a new client. Maybe that rocky point will come when you must deliver bad news about a snag or delay in the delivered work. Whatever the cause, a challenging conversation must occur. It is much more likely you will be able to maintain or even strengthen your connection with that client if you've started with a good relationship as a foundation.

In the absence of a good relationship in the beginning, all that's left is a transaction. Anything can go wrong in a transaction, and invariably does. If there is little to no relational connective tissue, then your engagement is at risk, even if you think all is well.

You don't have to be best friends, by the way. But if the thought of inviting someone to your home for a couple of hours for dinner gives you pause, wondering what your spouse might think, and questioning how you'll fill up that conversation time, then you should think twice about engaging that prospect.

Bad-Fit Clients

To be a successful solopreneur, you must learn how to say no to clients who are not a good fit for you. Even if you think you need the revenue—and your spouse tells you that you do—you may be saying yes to a situation that will end up costing you more trouble, money, and time than you ever imagined. Because you are so drained by a client who is not a good match, you may lose out on better opportunities which are right around the corner. Finally, this bad-fit client may start referring other clients just like them. That's certainly a situation you want to avoid.

Your business is just that—a business—not a hobby. To run a successful business, you must learn to recognize clients who are ideal for you and have the courage to say no to those who are not. This takes strategy, attentiveness, and practice. In fact, it's something even I had to learn the hard way.

When Rich called me with his desperate plea to help him with his monthly accounting, I was happy to see how I could help. As a franchisee of an established home services company, his business was taking off and he couldn't keep up with the bookkeeping and royalty reports he was required to file every month.

I went over to his house on his designated administrative day and found his dining room table almost completely covered, end to end, with papers: proposals, contracts, brochures, bank records, invoices, and bills. If we hadn't been talking, we probably would have heard the table groaning under the weight.

"It's something, isn't it?" he observed with a slight chuckle.

"Yes," I agreed, wondering what this scene would look like without an administrative day each week. "I guess your wife has given up on having anyone over for dinner," I added.

I asked the questions necessary to understand the business, define the problem, and then see whether his needs fit the solutions I offered. He was a talker, and before I knew it I had been there more than two hours. After all that time, I still didn't know how deep this guy's black hole of accounting was. Finally, I explained all the work we would have to do to get everything up to date, then I pulled a figure out of the air, which I thought would cover the clean-up job it would take to get him up to date.

He released a long sigh, and slowly his eyes went from stack to stack, all the way to the far end of the table from where he was sitting. "OK," he finally said. "Meet me here next week at the same time and bring an agreement for me to sign. Let's get going."

The following week, I sent Rich an email to confirm the meeting time we'd agreed to. Just a few minutes after I sent the email, he called me.

"John, please remind me why we are meeting tomorrow."

I suppressed my first reaction of, "Are you kidding me?" I could see, though, a huge imaginary red warning flag flapping in the wind. I reminded him that he had asked me to come back with an engagement agreement so we could get moving on his books and get everything caught up.

"About that," he said. "I've been talking to a $20-an-hour bookkeeper, and . . ." What he said after that really didn't sink in, as I completely glazed over.

After he stopped talking, I took a breath and then made the one correct move I made in this entire affair.

"You know what I think you need to do, Rich? You need to go with the $20-an-hour bookkeeper," I said. "You and I are not a good fit."

I went on to add that it was clear that a low price was really his only consideration. Further, I explained, I was a professional and my charge was worth it. I would deliver more value to him in helping him to better operate his business and make more money. I could bring my network to bear on his business, helping him make connections that would build his business and provide a healthy return on his investment with me. Eventually, I wished him well in his business, and we said our goodbyes.

As I reflected later on this situation, I realized that there were two critical mistakes I made.

1. First, I didn't control the initial interview. I didn't ask the questions necessary to understand this owner. I let him talk too much without me asking questions early on to understand whether we would be a good fit. Asking the right questions in a value conversation, particularly about price sensitivity, is crucial in an initial client interview. Allowing him to go on and on about his problems without explaining the solutions I could bring to his business was a failure on my part.

2. I did not grasp what he valued in accounting services, and second, I did not fully explain my value, either. Had I done these two things effectively, one of two results would have occurred. He would have either understood my value and the price I stated, or he would have revealed in his reactions that price was really his first consideration. I never got the conversation to this key point.

The one thing I did correctly was exercise the courage not to waste any more time on the situation. He needed to be free to pursue what he wanted, and I obviously needed to move on.

Bad-fit clients come in a range of personalities. Most are easy to spot, others, not so much. Your ability to spot them could mean the difference between enjoying the transformation you bring to clients you relish working with, and hating it every single day you power on your laptop. That said, here are a few bad-fit client personalities you should be aware of, tips on how to spot them, and suggestions on how to avoid engaging with them.

The Tire Kicker

These people just want to test the water. They are shopping around and don't really know what they want. If the conversation you have with them goes too far below their surface-level inquiry, they have very vague answers or none at all. They do not have a firm sense of the outcomes they're looking for, and because of that, they can't express a timeline for completion of the project. It is possible you might be able to help if you take the The Generosity Mindset approach and engage the tire kicker in a more strategic, higher-altitude conversation in which you attempt to uncover wider needs. Often, however, tire kickers are resistant to such entreaties, and you will have to be content with telling them you're happy to chat when they have a better idea of what they're looking for.

The DIYer

These people would rather do it themselves, but they want the blueprints of your knowledge and insights so they can continue to push off hiring an expert. That expert they want to avoid hiring, of course, just happens to be you. They are simultaneously hoping that you're too dumb to figure that out but smart enough in your discipline to help them.

At a certain point in the conversation, you must draw a line by saying something along the lines of, "I have clients who pay me to work on exactly what you are asking, and it wouldn't be fair to them if I continue with this free consultation. I'm happy to chat about whether it might make sense for us to work together in a client-service provider relationship." A statement like this brings the conversation to a crescendo of either a shift toward dialogue on how you can work with them, or, more likely, a polite end to the conversation.

The Brain Picker

This person wants to pick your brain for as long as you will allow them, find out what you know, get some free advice, then go about their way. The brain picker may be a DIYer, but they can also be someone who hasn't decided on what actions they need to take and are in analysis paralysis mode. They waste your time, trying to make you think they want to hire you, but instead engage in endless conversations and run around in circles if you allow it.

As with the DIYer, an effective way to bring the conversation to a tipping point is to let the individual know, in a nice way, that you have clients that pay for the ground they are asking you to cover at no charge. It's unfair to them for you to go further without entering into a paying engagement.

The Know-It-All

The know-it-all is the person who calls you up, seemingly with an interest in your services, but ends up monopolizing the conversation with their own knowledge and accomplishments. The know-it-all is not really seeking your help. Underneath the confident front they're putting up, down deep they are actually quite uncertain and afraid. They don't want help; on the contrary, they crave affirmation of what they've already decided. They are un-coachable and unwilling to learn or even listen. If you spend enough time talking to them, they might even argue with you.

Don't waste your time. Let them know that you're not a great fit for them simply because they already seem to have all the answers to their problems.

The Cheapskate

Like Rich in the example above, this person is only looking for the lowest price, not the best value or solution. The cheapskates often reveal themselves very quickly. Within the first few questions they ask about your rates. Your answer to this question should simply be that you don't know the answer to the question until you're able to have a deeper conversation with them about the uniqueness of their situation and the solutions you would recommend. If they persist, then they're almost certainly a price shopper.

In this case, you have two choices, depending on your personality and how spicy you're feeling that day. You can simply tell them that you don't think the two of you will be a good fit, and that you're willing to recommend another services provider to help them. They will ask why you came to that conclusion, and the best answer is to simply say, without any aggravation, that they seem more interested in a transaction than a relationship, and that in your business you value relationships.

The other option you could employ is to take the highest possible engagement value any client would pay you (whether you have that engagement or not), multiply it by three or four, and then tell them something like this: "Some clients will pay as much as $ (whatever number applies to you) for the full scope of what we can provide. I highly doubt that applies to you. In fact, I suspect the fee might be much lower. (If that's what you guess.) I won't know a more precise range, however, until we can have a deeper conversation about the specifics of your needs."

What you've done with this answer is create a very high price anchor, one that makes any other pricing discussed afterward, assuming you get that far, seem like a relative bargain. If the individual is indeed a cheapskate, though, this answer will scare them to death, and they'll disengage from you as quickly as they're able to run, thankfully for you.

The Barterer

The barterer might also be the cheapskate, but not necessarily. The barterer is the person who wants to trade services with no cash changing hands. A website developer, for example, might propose to build a new website for an accountant in exchange for bookkeeping services.

Bartering rarely works out well for both parties. Invariably, one side, or possibly both, feels that they aren't getting enough value out of the trade. That's not too surprising, because the terms of the barter are rarely, if ever, made based on the value of client outcomes. On the contrary, a barter is usually made based on number of hours or some other measure irrelevant to realized client value.

Your response to the service provider who wants to barter for your services is simple: You don't do it. Tell them you will consider it when someone figures out how you can pay for the utilities with services.

Friends and Family

There are some family members you would go to the ends of the earth for. You might leap at the chance to help a child or a grandchild with their business, for example, which might be one of the most satisfying actions you ever do. That is not what I'm referring to here. On the contrary, I'm alluding to those family members and long-time friends who love the fact that you do what you do, and they believe because they have known you for so long, you will be more than happy to help them, either at a highly reduced rate or for free. These are the family members or friends who make your teeth grind when you think ahead to the next time you'll see them.

You must enter such a conversation with these family members understanding the idea that the pain of saying no on the front end, as difficult as you might think that is, is actually much less than the long-term pain of dealing with an engagement that goes sour.

You are guaranteed, along with everyone else in attendance, to hear about the latter for years to come at Thanksgiving. To avoid these engagements of misery, your best option is generally to state simply that you are not the best fit for the type of engagement their situation requires. You would waste their time and resources, as well as their money, assuming they are offering to pay you in hard currency and not just with Grandma's molasses cookies. You must convince them that the pain they'll endure is much greater than the price savings they assume they'll realize from hiring you.

Rude and Unkind People

People who are brusque and disrespectful are generally very easy to spot at the front end of any interaction. If you wanted to work with such individuals, you wouldn't have left your corporate job. Why would you even consider putting up with them in a business you own and call all the shots? Tell them you are not a great fit and make up the reason if you must. Tell them that you're at capacity and aren't accepting new clients now. Wish them the best and send them on their way. If you refer them to another services provider, give your colleague the courtesy of a heads up on why the referral is coming their way. They'll appreciate your honesty and that you are looking out for them.

All these types of clients can cause headaches and take up an inordinate amount of your time. Don't fall for any of it. Your avoidance of such clients is not just about protecting yourself. On the contrary, I don't consider it to be a selfish act but, assuming you're not mean about it, one that springs from The Generosity Mindset.

The reason is because when you knowingly take on a bad-fit client, you will come to resent that client over time. You'll secretly be angry at them when it was you who overlooked the poor fit and took them on as a client. You won't give them the best service, and that's not in their best interest. The relationship will deteriorate, and you'll eventually end up with a former client who has nothing good to say about you.

That is not in your interest or theirs.

Great-Fit Clients

As with bad-fit clients, clients who are a great fit for you come in a variety of personalities and traits, depending on the nature of your business and your services discipline. For example, a professional organizer will have unique questions for their prospects in a value conversation, and be listening for different indicators, than will a business attorney.

That said, here are several traits and indicators of a great-fit client which generally apply across the board:

The Investor

Investors are business owners who understand the concept of return on investment and operate their business accordingly. They view their expenditures as investments that are meant to deliver a return, rather than sunk costs. The return they are looking for could be in the form of additional revenue or expense savings. The best investors also view intangible returns, such as time savings for themselves and their team, as having extremely high value. These clients are ideal because they will understand the need for a value conversation that allows them to identify the tangible and intangible value you can deliver (return) relative to your fee (their investment).

The Exasperated

An exasperated client is one who is tired of the status quo and is ready to get unstuck and go in a different direction. Their anxiety for a solution to their issues overwhelms whatever do-it-yourself or cheapskate tendencies they might have been affected by previously. You will get a sense of the level of exasperation by the speed with which they want to get to "what's next?" Their level of exasperation may cause them to be impatient with the value conversation you are seeking to have with them. In such cases, you will need to explain that while you understand their desire for a solution, the questions you're asking are necessary for you to craft high-value solutions for them.

The Decision Maker

Quite simply, this client is done with dawdling around hoping a problem will go away, attempting a solution on their own, or some other delay tactic. They are ready to make a decision, and often they are so ready they'll tell you so. If they don't tell you themselves, when you ask them what's needed for them to make a decision to engage you, they will have a ready answer.

Friends and Family

These individuals are those among your friends and family who, unlike the friends and family who want special treatment, are those who are perfectly happy being treated just like any other client you have. They understand that they are helping you build a better business. They're giving you a learning laboratory that will help you improve. They expect you to do the work, of course, but they'll give you more latitude to correct mistakes and set things right if needed.

A word of warning: Don't take advantage of their good-heartedness by giving them any less service than what you'd offer to any other client. Give them the same great value and service, if not something extra, that you'd give to any other client. After all, they're helping you with more than just revenue.

The Grace-Filled

I don't mean those clients who have great dance steps. I'm referring to clients who are full of enough grace to understand that you are a human being and not a machine. They understand that you need time away from your work to recharge because that time of rejuvenation helps them. They will ask how you are doing and sincerely mean it. Arguably even more important, they will ask how your spouse or your family are. They'll never call you at 6 a.m. on Sunday unless it's in your scope of service or they truly have an emergency. The grace-filled are a delight to work with because they operate with The Generosity Mindset themselves.

You will never have a perfect set of clients. Everyone is human and has their quirks and their own bad days. Clients who are a great fit for you and your business, however, have a lot less of those foibles.

Great-fit clients bring joy to your business. They pick you up when you're having a tough day or are down on yourself for some reason. They appreciate you. They deliver value back to you that goes well beyond whatever revenue they account for in your practice.

Why would you settle for clients who don't give you such incalculable value?

Everyone is Not Your Client

You are not so brilliant that you have all the answers for everyone who crosses your path. Neither am I. You don't have such a dynamic personality that you'll get along with any and every client who comes your way. (Me either.) "Everyone" is not your client and really, you don't want and cannot serve everyone.

Some people don't want to invest in being helped. Maybe they're not happy with their present dysfunction, but they're content enough that they are not motivated to change. Others don't want to be helped because they think they have it all figured out. Sometimes, all you can do for clients like this is say, "Bless your heart" as they hurtle toward the cliff. Some prospects have an extremely low perceived value of what you do. You might convince some of them to change their mind, but for many of them, you won't. That's ok. Don't take it personally or view it as a reflection of the quality of what you do.

As discussed in Chapter 4 on positioning, when you attempt to appeal to everyone, you appeal to no one. Further, there is no way, however smart and capable you are, that you can possibly serve every client who comes your way. Even the subset of clients who are good fits for you aren't all the same. Some have limited budgets or just want to try you out in a smaller scale engagement. Others might have severe issues that you are perfectly suited to address. They see you as that ideal solution and want to engage you in a comprehensive scope in order to bring transformation to their business as quickly as they can get it.

This variety of client perspectives and values is why I advocate moving away from a single price, single service model to "good, better, best" engagement options. Offering such options is a recognition that different clients have different needs, desires, goals, and concerns.

We'll dive deeper into crafting engagement options in Chapter 8, but here's a preview.

The "good" version of your engagement options is your most basic service offering of what's been requested by the client. It is the basic, plain vanilla version of your work which all clients need at a minimum.

The "better" version is an upgrade with more features. It appeals to clients with slightly deeper pockets and a broader vision for what their outcomes and results should be. They value and desire more of your services than the "good" group, but there is another level of engagement they are still not quite ready for.

The "best" version is your premium, "white glove" service offering. It is the full range of what you're able to offer those clients who want a complete experience of your work.

You cannot physically get to everyone who needs the transformation you offer. So don't get caught up in thinking that everyone is your customer. It's just not true. You don't want that anyway. Even with the clients whom you deem a good fit, each has different perceptions of value, and, therefore, varying ideas of the services they want to purchase from you.

The Three Choices You Have in Dealing with a Bad-Fit Client

You have taken all the precautions. You've learned from your past experiences and those of others. Despite all that, you have a few bad-fit clients on your hands. Sometimes as humans we get stuck in the status quo. It is easier to let things roll along with an unpleasant situation than to deal with it. This is why people don't go to the doctor when they have an unusual pain. The same applies to bad-fit clients—you hope the pain will go away, but as the old saying goes, "Hope is not a strategy." When dealing with such a client, you have three choices.

First, you could do nothing. If you decide on inertia, then be honest with yourself and acknowledge that doing nothing is actually a decision. You are making the choice to say yes to the situation you find yourself in and the dysfunction it creates for both you and the client. If you do nothing, your frustration will grow, and eventually that frustration will boil over in an unpleasant way. You are no different than any other human being. Unresolved frustrations eventually express themselves in some way. That's the way we humans are wired. You will take it out on the dog, your spouse, your kid, or even that client. Maybe, if it's bad enough, all of the above. No, the pain will not go away. On the contrary, it will get worse.

The second option is to adjust your pricing upward to account for the aggravation factor. Think about what it's worth to you to cover the tangible costs (extra employee time, materials, and so forth) and the intangible costs to you (your own frustration, poor employee morale, the opportunity costs of working on that client project versus something else you could be doing). Decide on a fee that covers those costs, and then add a healthy premium to that figure. The resulting figure should make you queasy. If it doesn't, it's probably not high enough.

The third option is simply to let that client go. If that's what you decide, do yourself and that client a favor. Take the high road. It's not about you or how much you've grown. It's about what is right for them. You are no longer the best fit for them, they need to find someone else who is, and you'll help them do that if they choose to accept your help. You will have freed yourself up to do even better work for those clients who are a better fit for you.

The second and third options work together, by the way. You give the client the power to select either option: continuing to work with you at the new, higher price, or finding another provider to work with. Just make sure that price is high enough that you are genuinely happy with either choice they make. Operating your practice on this basis represents The Generosity Mindset in action.

Using The Generosity Mindset to Diagnose Clients

Your ability to diagnose clients starts with whether they are a good fit for your practice. Even with those clients where each of you agree that you want to work together, varying perceptions of value exist. It's in the best interest of everyone you meet, whether a client or not, that you successfully diagnose their needs using a value conversation. This is the best way to determine whether you are the appropriate professional for them, and if so, to offer different ways to work together.

You will simultaneously heap generosity on yourself and your business and you'll have better-fit clients who you consider a joy to work with. An essential aspect of that joy, however, is effectively pricing your services, which we'll discuss in the next section.

PART 2

PRICING STRATEGY

CHAPTER 7

HOW YOU PRICE IS CRITICAL
TO YOUR SUCCESS

In the Introduction, I pointed to famed investor Warren Buffett and his comments on the importance of pricing in assessing a business:

> "The single most important decision in evaluating a business is pricing power. If you've got the power to raise prices without losing business to a competitor, you've got a very good business. And if you have to have a prayer session before raising the price by 10 percent, then you've got a terrible business."

The quote, powerful on its own, is even more insightful when you look at it in context. Buffett's comments on pricing power came out of testimony he gave to the Financial Crisis Inquiry Commission (FCIC). This Congressionally-appointed body was charged with investigating the causes of the financial crisis of 2007-2010. One of the targets of their investigation was Moody's Investors Service, one of the dominant players in the business of rating securities. Ratings agencies Moody's and Standard & Poor's had conferred AAA ratings on mortgage-backed securities and other instruments, which turned out to be a major source of financial losses during the crisis.

Buffett's Berkshire Hathaway held 15% of Moody's shares when Moody's went public in 2000. By 2008, its ownership had risen to 20%; by 2010, Berkshire Hathaway and three other investors owned more than 50% of Moody's shares.

When the role of Moody's in the financial crisis was examined by the FCIC, therefore, Buffett became a source of interest. He was questioned by FCIC counsel Bradley Bondi, and Buffett discussed the rationale for his Moody's investment:

Buffett: " . . . Basically, the single-most important decision in evaluating a business is pricing power. If you've got the power to raise prices without losing business to a competitor, you've got a very good business. And if you have to have a prayer session before raising the price by a tenth of a cent, then you've got a terrible business. I've been in both, and I know the difference."

Bondi: "Now, you've described the importance of quality management in your investing decisions, and I know your mentor, Benjamin Graham—I happen to have read his book as well—has described the importance of management. What attracted you to the management of Moody's when you made your initial investments?"

Buffett: "I knew nothing about the management of Moody's. . . . I've also said many times in reports and elsewhere that when a management with reputation for brilliance gets hooked up with a business with a reputation for bad economics, it's the reputation of the business that remains intact.

"If you've got a good enough business, if you have a monopoly newspaper, if you have a network television station—I'm talking of the past—you know, your idiot nephew could run it. And if you've got a really good business, it doesn't make any difference . . . "

Very few of us will ever develop a business with a dominant position like Moody's. The point Buffett is making about Moody's, though, applies to all businesses, large and small: How you price your product or service is critically important to the success of your enterprise.

There is comfort here for you as a business owner. Maybe your operating processes aren't optimal. Your lead conversion might be off. Your expenses may be higher than they should be. There is a lot that can go wrong in a business, but excellence in pricing covers many errors.

You don't have to be a Harvard MBA or the best marketer or a particularly eloquent speaker. Your expenses do not need to be the lowest in your industry. Your business doesn't need to be the biggest or be a household name. You don't have to have the largest share of the market.

If you develop a business with pricing power, you win. It's that simple. The pricing strategies that follow cover other mistakes you will inevitably make in your business. When you price to the value of the client outcomes you are generating, you operate from a mindset of abundance. You'll be searching for ways to aid the client on their journey in ways they didn't expect, and when you do that, you cement the relationship.

The Accounting of Pricing

If you are not into numbers, you may be tempted to skip the next few pages. Please don't. It's vital that you understand the effect pricing and changes in price can have on your income statement.

The fastest and most effective way of changing your bottom line is to increase your prices. This statement is not my opinion. It is an accounting fact. This basic law of accounting demands that you make pricing a central strategy behind how you run your business.

While there are several ways to increase your revenue, no other option is as reliable with as low a risk as optimizing your pricing. To compare, you could hire a business development professional. What if you make the wrong hire? Even if you do select the right person, that individual will take time to get up to speed and generate results that hit your bottom line. In the meantime, you have an investment in their salary and other expenses they generate which you'll have to cover.

Maybe you could spend more on marketing. If you did, then you must worry about whether you are utilizing the right marketing strategy, and if you are, you must wait for the results of that strategy to pay off.

When you increase prices, on the other hand, there is very little lag-time to receive the benefit of that change. You don't have to spend money to make money, like you do with staffing additions or changes to sales or to marketing. You certainly don't have the same amount of risk that you do with those two alternatives to increasing revenue.

To illustrate the power of pricing for a solopreneur, consider a hypothetical business, Sheila's Professional Organizing Business. Sheila has built a nice business. She has a healthy bottom line after taxes, which gives her more than six figures of bottom-line profit each year to either reinvest in the business or to pay out to herself as the owner.

SHEILA'S PROFESSIONAL ORGANIZING BUSINESS
INCOME STATEMENT

Revenue	$500,000
Variable Costs	$100,000
Gross Profit	$400,000
Fixed Costs	
Personnell	$125,000
Marketing	$ 50,000
Rent/Utilities	$ 45,000
Other	$ 15,000
Total Fixed Costs	$235,000
Pre-Tax Profit	$165,000
Tax Rate	35%
Income Taxes	$57,750
Net Income	$107,250
Net Profit Margin	21.5%

Now let's say Sheila decides she wants to grow the business. She decides that she is going to offer a 15% discount on her services with the hope of increasing her clients by 15%. Let's see what happens:

SHEILA'S PROFESSIONAL ORGANIZING BUSINESS
INCOME STATEMENT
(AFTER A 15% PRICE REDUCTION TO WIN 15% MORE CLIENTS)

	Before	After	%Change
Revenue	$500,000	$488,750	-2.3%
Variable Costs	$100,000	$115,000	15.0%
Gross Profit	$400,000	$373,750	-6.6%
Fixed Costs			
Personnell	$125,000	$125,000	
Marketing	$ 50,000	$ 50,000	
Rent/Utilities	$ 45,000	$ 45,000	
Other	$ 15,000	$ 15,000	
Total Fixed Costs	$235,000	$235,000	
Pre-Tax Profit	$165,000	$165,000	-15.9%
Tax Rate	35%	35%	
Income Taxes	$57,750	$48,563	
Net Income	$107,250	$90,188	-15.9%
Net Profit Margin	21.5%	18.5%	

Let's assume that Sheila's strategy works perfectly and that she realizes her goal of 15% more clients because of the 15% price decrease.

Contrary to what you might expect, Sheila's revenue does not increase. When you apply the discount pricing to her original clients, revenue on the existing client base drops by $75,000 to $425,000. She gains 15% more clients, so the effect of the new clients is an additional $63,750 in revenue ($425,000 in revenue, plus 15% additional clients or $63,750, equals $488,750). The net change in revenue, therefore, is a decline of 2.3%, from $500,000 to $488,750.

We're assuming, for the moment, that Sheila actually pulls in 15% additional clients because of the price discount. There are many reasons to believe this strategy will fail, as discounts, in and of themselves, do not attract additional clients. (I'll explain why later.) For now, though, let's assume Sheila's strategy has the intended outcome.

Note that variable costs are based on client volume, whereas fixed costs are not, so we've separated the two. Sheila's variable costs, because she has 15% more clients, goes up by 15%. The net effect on her gross margin is a decline of $26,250, or 6.6%. The fixed costs don't change because those additional costs are not affected by volume.

After she pays taxes, Sheila's net income has declined by almost 16%, or $17,062. That's $17,062 less than otherwise could be reinvested in the business or put into her pocket as the owner. Sheila has placed her business in a weaker position because of this strategy.

Now let's assume instead that Sheila decides to raise her prices by 10%:

SHEILA'S PROFESSIONAL ORGANIZING BUSINESS
INCOME STATEMENT
(AFTER A 10% PRICE INCREASE WITH NO LOSS IN CLIENTS)

	Before	After	%Change
Revenue	$500,000	$550,000	10.0%
Variable Costs	$100,000	$100,000	0.0%
Gross Profit	$400,000	$450,000	12.5%
Fixed Costs			
Personnell	$125,000	$125,000	
Marketing	$ 50,000	$ 50,000	
Rent/Utilities	$ 45,000	$ 45,000	
Other	$ 15,000	$ 15,000	
Total Fixed Costs	$235,000	$235,000	
Pre-Tax Profit	$165,000	$215,000	30.3%
Tax Rate	35%	35%	
Income Taxes	$57,750	$72,250	
Net Income	$107,250	$139,750	30.3%
Net Profit Margin	21.5%	25.4%	

There is no change in variable costs, because Sheila has the same number of clients (volume) as before. Her fixed costs, as before, stay the same.

After she pays taxes, Sheila's net income has increased by more than 30%. That's an additional $32,500 in net income which she has available to fund additional business growth or to receive as distributions to her as the owner.

Now let's assume that Sheila is convinced of the power of price changes to increase her bottom line, but she's a little timid and scared of doing too much. It's a fear I see consistently with the clients I work with.

Here's a scenario in which Sheila increases her prices by only 3%, well below the rate of inflation as I write these words:

SHEILA'S PROFESSIONAL ORGANIZING BUSINESS
INCOME STATEMENT
(AFTER A 3% PRICE INCREASE WITH NO LOSS IN CLIENTS)

	Before	After	%Change
Revenue	$500,000	$515,000	3.0%
Variable Costs	$100,000	$100,000	0.0%
Gross Profit	$400,000	$415,000	3.8%
Fixed Costs			
Personnell	$125,000	$125,000	
Marketing	$ 50,000	$ 50,000	
Rent/Utilities	$ 45,000	$ 45,000	
Other	$ 15,000	$ 15,000	
Total Fixed Costs	$235,000	$235,000	
Pre-Tax Profit	$165,000	$180,000	9.1%
Tax Rate	35%	35%	
Income Taxes	$57,750	$63,000	
Net Income	$107,250	$117,000	9.1%
Net Profit Margin	21.5%	22.7%	

Even with only a 3% price increase, Sheila has increased the profit in her business by more than 9%, or approximately $10,000. For Sheila, this should be an easy decision to make, as the risk is negligible that any of her clients will complain or avoid her business because of such a small increase in price.

Let's consider one more scenario, one which is quite bold and intended to open your mind to what is possible with a thoughtful pricing strategy.

Assume that Sheila decides she only wants to work with her very best-fit clients, the ones who she delivers the most value for and those who most value her and her company's services. Sheila decides to raise her pricing by 30%, knowing she will lose 30% of her clients. The clients she anticipates losing are those who are more price sensitive and are more difficult to work with.

Here is the effect of this decision on her income statement:

SHEILA'S PROFESSIONAL ORGANIZING BUSINESS INCOME STATEMENT (AFTER A 30% PRICE INCREASE WITH A 30% REDUCTION IN CLIENTS)			
	Before	After	%Change
Revenue	$500,000	$650,000	30.0%
Variable Costs	$100,000	$70,000	-30.0%
Gross Profit	$400,000	$580,000	3.8%
Fixed Costs			
Personnell	$125,000	$125,000	
Marketing	$ 50,000	$ 50,000	
Rent/Utilities	$ 45,000	$ 45,000	
Other	$ 15,000	$ 15,000	
Total Fixed Costs	$235,000	$235,000	
Pre-Tax Profit	$165,000	$345,000	109.1%
Tax Rate	35%	35%	
Income Taxes	$57,750	$120,750	
Net Income	$107,250	$224,750	109.1%
Net Profit Margin	21.5%	34.5%	

But what if my assumptions are wrong? Even if they are, note how much leeway exists in which to be wrong! Even if Sheila doesn't realize as much savings from fewer clients or the revenue she expected from her price increase, she is still much better off.

Whatever decision Sheila makes with her business, she has one of the most important possessions any solopreneur can have in their business: choices. She can scale, merge in other small businesses, or open new locations. She can decide, alternatively, that she is ready to dial back the effort a bit, maybe travel and play with the grandkids, but she's not ready to retire. Whatever she decides, the decision is hers alone.

That's what effective pricing in your business does for you. It gives you choices.

Whatever services business you have, run your own scenarios. Have your bookkeeper or business advisor help you, if necessary. I guarantee that you'll confirm what Warren Buffett said about pricing, that how you price is a crucial lever in the growth of your business.

The Problems with Hourly Pricing

There are many problems with hourly pricing, both for clients and for you as the services provider. Pricing by time is rife with conflicts, causes misleading assumptions, and can even lead to disagreements and misunderstandings between you and the client.

Some of the negative issues hourly billing causes for clients include:

- An hourly rate is not the final cost of the project or engagement. When you quote your hourly rate, that is not a price. An hourly rate is a single input in calculating a final price. Clients do not know the hours involved in doing whatever you do, particularly as the complexity of the project grows. If they are forced to guess, they invariably guess on the low side, and are subsequently surprised when they see the final invoice, the number of hours, and the amount due.

- Clients hate "surprise bills." Related to the point above, clients don't know how long it takes to do the work you do; they always guess low on what a bill will be when based on hours. When they open the invoice, they are surprised, and the relationship potentially sours.

- Clients hate nit-picky bills. Ask a client what they think about a bill they got from their now former attorney, for example, who billed telephone calls in six-minute increments.

- Your hourly rate takes the focus away from what's most important: **the value of outcomes you deliver.** Assume, for example, that you are quoting on a project that will deliver a total of $1 million in cost savings to a company, and that it will take you ten hours to complete your project. If you only quote them an hourly rate, you might quote them $10,000 an hour, which would represent a compelling investment for that client ($10,000/hour times 10 hours equals a $100,000 fee to earn $1,000,000 in cost savings. That's a great investment!). If you quote $10,000 an hour, however, the first reaction from your client will likely be an expletive followed by, "I don't make anywhere near $10,000 an hour; what makes you think you're worth anywhere near that?!?"

- Because the client doesn't know the full cost of the project, they cannot budget or plan effectively. Even if you offer an estimated high-low range of the final project cost, an estimate does not represent the final number on the invoice. Clients know this.

- Pricing by time creates a conflict that is not in the best interest of the client. The client wants a project completed not only successfully but also as quickly as they can get it. The faster you complete a project, the less you will make. What a terribly perverse incentive.

- Clients don't call you when they should. When you bill by the hour, a client is more hesitant to call you when confronted with a problem. That's exactly when you want them to call you. Otherwise, they wait until that small problem mushrooms into a serious emergency in which the solutions become harder and more expensive. As the services provider, hourly billing creates several significant negatives for you, your relationships with your clients, and your ability to deliver significant value to them.

- Your pricing is based on inputs, not on the value you help create. Clients care about the outcomes of your work and the value of those outcomes. That's what they want to pay for. Imagine going into an Italian restaurant and asking how much the large pepperoni pizza costs. What would you do if the owner quoted you the price of pepperonis? The pepperonis are only one input for the pizza. Not only that, but the number of pepperonis doesn't place any value on the quality of the ingredients, the ambience of the restaurant, its level of service, or any other aspect of the dining experience, all of which, taken together, comprise the full value the customer receives.

- Pricing by the hour leads to your service being viewed as a commodity. You are judged more like a can of dog food than the professional you are.

- You get penalized for your expertise. The faster you successfully complete the work, the less you make.

- You won't bill for all the hours you work. You won't because you'll look at your timesheet and start convincing yourself that your client will be surprised and angry, so you preemptively take hours off the invoice.

- You won't get paid for all the hours you've billed. When the client gets surprised by the bill, your first reaction is typically to trim back the hours you'll accept payment for even further.

- Pricing by the hour, by definition, mismatches the revenue and expenses associated with an engagement. You don't get paid until after, often well after, hours are expended and associated project expenses are incurred.

- Pricing by the hour limits your income. There are only so many hours in the day. You can't invent or manufacture any more than what you have now unless you start cheating by fudging client bills.

In his book *The Infinite Game*, Simon Sinek shares a story about his experience with hourly billing and the distortions it caused. While working at a large advertising agency that began using time sheets to log billable hours, Sinek essentially ignored the process, going months without tracking his time. When he was called on his insubordination, he acquiesced and got with the plan. Once he began completing his time sheets, he shockingly realized how often he would come in early and leave late, adding substantial hours to his project. He assumed the reason the time sheets were implemented at the agency was due to some billing issue in accounting or because a client wanted proof of who was clocking the most hours for their project.

Was the problem really in the accounting department? No, the problem arose because of a billing method which invites inaccuracies, abuse, and worse. According to Sinek, his time sheets were fiction because he had previously underestimated the amount of time he spent on client projects. That led to underbilling, not overbilling clients. The flaws in hourly billing don't always cheat the client; they often cheat you as the professional sending out the bill.

This is one reason I tell professional services providers that if they are billing by the hour, by definition they are underpricing their services.

You might ask how underbilling with a time-based billing method can shortchange the client. The problem is simple. When the client gets that bill, they don't necessarily know that all the hours aren't billed. An invoice based on time invites questions like:

- Did this work really take that much time?
- Why does this person think they're so special that they get to charge this much per hour? (They're wondering this about you.)

- Can I trust that the previous bills I paid were right? Future ones? Will they try to make it back on me?

All these questions are misdirected. None of them address the most central point: Did I, as the client, receive more value than what I paid in fees? Because the bill focuses attention on inputs that have nothing to do with value received, clients may start questioning a services provider who is actually providing great value.

Hourly billing is ill-advised and misguided because it cheats both the client and the services provider, often simultaneously.

Discount Your Way to a Poor Reputation

When a solopreneur starts their services business, the default pricing decision, almost invariably, is to discount their services because the business is new. They will figure out what others are charging—usually an hourly rate—and discount heavily based on what they learn. It's a terrible way to begin.

It is an understandable decision, but one that's based on the flawed idea that your discounted services will bring in clients who ordinarily will not engage you because your business is brand new. I did it myself when I started out, but the problem is that it often leads to long-term problems for your business. Sure, you might attract a few takers who are exclusively focused on price, but those buyers are typically not your ideal clients. These clients often expect you to give them champagne services even though they paid the rot gut beer price.

For clients who are judging a services provider based on both price and their perceived value of the service, you have created an anchoring problem. All of us are prone to a cognitive bias known as "anchoring" when it comes to determining whether to make a purchase based on the information we initially encounter. This starting point, or "anchor price," influences a client's view of the product's value.

Subsequent decisions are then skewed by the initial reference price. These decisions can be entirely arbitrary and unrelated to the value of the item. Subsequent price points are evaluated relative to the price anchor, not the value of the service. That is often the case even if the perceived value of the service, in that client's mind, is quite high.

When you discount, you have "anchored low." It's virtually impossible to get that discounted price out of the heads of those who have been exposed to your so-called "introductory" price. Any price you charge after the introductory period is judged relative to the discount price you started with.

Here is an illustration of the power of anchoring. I have a subscription to *The Athletic*, an online sports journalism site. Early on, when the site was new, I took advantage of their promotional pricing offer of $1 a month. Several months later, they let me know that I would have to pay the normal price of $9.99 a month.

I cancelled. The $1 price was fixed in my head. There was no way, I thought, that the site was worth $120 a year, based on the other subscriptions I had and what I'd seen on *The Athletic*'s site during the promotional period. I made that decision even though a lot of comparable sites were priced similarly. I have since been lured back as a subscriber. Why? Because they offered me the original $1 per month price I paid at the beginning. For this site, the $1 a month is cemented in my head.

It's extremely difficult to get a low-price anchor out of the head of the typical client. Moreover, it can cause you serious harm in your business if your reputation starts to solidify as the cheap option for your service. It damages your brand, as your price is a marketing signal. Based on how you set your pricing, the signal clients detect can be one of inferiority. (It works the other way, too: your pricing can exude signals of quality.)

You may think you can discount here and there, and clients won't compare notes. You're wrong. Clients find out, and word gets around about whether you're a cheap provider. Once you start discounting, it can be hard to stop. You justify a discount for your twentieth client, for instance, because you handled the previous nineteen the same way. After a while, your practice becomes a dull blade.

The good news is that you can reorient your practice. If you've just gone out on your own or are about to start your practice, however, it is much better to avoid a change of blades caused by poor pricing.

Pro-bono Work

While I was speaking with a solopreneur bookkeeper about her business and her pricing strategy, she told me that she had several friends who needed help when they started their businesses and she had offered to do their books at a heavily discounted rate. These arrangements were still in place after several years.

"Do you deliver your completed work for them at the same time you do for your other clients?" I asked.

"Yes, more or less," she replied.

"And they've come to expect that because of the fine service you've given them, right?"

"Yes."

"And how are their businesses doing now?" I asked.

"They've done well," she said.

"And they haven't volunteered to pay your normal rate now that they've got established businesses, have they?"

We both laughed because I already knew the answer.

Offering to work with friends and family at a discounted rate or worse, for free, can eat into your profits, particularly if the discount extends beyond a one-time offer into an ongoing and expected practice. This bookkeeper had spoiled her friends with a premium service offering which they had come to expect as customary. Because she had never insisted they pay her actual rates, those friends had forgotten that they were paying discounted rates.

No matter the service you provide, friends and family will find a way to ease into your practice with the request for a discount. Most often, discounting for friends is not beneficial for them or for you.

There are some clear reasons why the "friends and family" discount can strike a blow to your business. While you're doing this work for your friends, an existing client relationship blows up because you haven't given them the level of service they expect for the normal price they're paying. Or a great new client comes along, and you can't take them on because you're too busy doing work for others pro-bono.

Initially, the discounts and the associated work look innocuous, but the seeds of dysfunction in your business are planted, waiting to grow. This problem is rampant with CPAs, accountants, and bookkeepers, but can also weave itself into the mix with videographers, social media strategists, coaches, writers, dog walkers, and other services providers.

I caught the disease once myself. A non-profit I had volunteered with and whose cause I strongly believe in needed some accounting work done. The previous professional handling the work had volunteered their time, and the work required wasn't tedious. I offered to do it at no charge because it was my contribution to a cause in which I believed. The work was easy and wouldn't take a lot of my time.

The problem, it turned out later, was that they wanted their work done at specific times which conflicted with the work I was doing for paying clients. I didn't go into the job with the understanding that they assumed I would deliver the work pretty much on demand. After a few months, we mutually agreed that they needed to seek another arrangement. We parted ways amicably, and I learned a valuable lesson about how and whether to do pro-bono or even discounted work.

Price and Perception: "Palessi" and Payless Shoes

A new shoe boutique, Palessi, opened in Santa Monica, California in a space formerly occupied by Armani. To celebrate the grand opening, Palessi threw a party for influencers.

As they drank champagne and snapped selfies for Instagram postings, the influencers were asked their opinions about the various shoes and boots and their willingness to pay the prices indicated. Using descriptions like "elegant" and "sophisticated," this group lauded the materials, style, and craftsmanship of the store's wares. They said they would pay a variety of prices, all in the hundreds of dollars. The top offer was $640, and Palessi sold about $3,000 worth of products in the first few hours of the party.

The big reveal at the party, as it turns out, was that this store was a pop-up stocked by Payless ShoeSource. All of what "Palessi" offered at the party was available at Payless Shoes for prices ranging from $19.99 to $39.99. You may chuckle at how this group got bamboozled, but everyone is subject to the same principle—that perception of quality and willingness to pay is heavily influenced by context, placement, or geography. We're all subject to it.

The "influencers" at Palessi were clearly willing to pay for location (a swanky store in Santa Monica), exclusivity (an invitation-only grand opening party), association (I'm part of the "in crowd."), acceptance (a purchase here validates my influencer status), and brand perception (Palessi? Must be Italian!). Even among this group, however, different individuals were willing to pay different prices, based on their own interpretation of the value of the sum of all these factors.

This principle is not just confined to retail. In the B2B and professional services space, think about a sloppily dressed lawyer who works out of a storefront. You can peer in and see him working at an old metal desk with an ancient computer. Then, consider the sharply dressed attorney in a downtown high-rise, sitting behind a large wooden desk, Apple computer at the ready, in a well-appointed office.

What's your perception of the quality of the legal advice you'll receive and the price you're willing to pay either of these attorneys?

If you are pricing your services without a keen understanding of the context of how clients view and understand your services, your price is wrong. You're almost certainly leaving profit on the table.

Context in Pricing: The Waffle House Edition

My son is a Waffle House fan and has been since he was old enough to know what a waffle is. He's twenty-three now.

His standard order, for a long time, involved a waffle. When he was preschool age, kids' waffles at Waffle House were a dollar. Kids' waffles with bacon are now $4.25, so this long-gone value was indeed quite a deal. If you have been to Waffle House, you know that all the waffles come out of the same sized griddle, which you can see, so it's no big secret. A kid's waffle, therefore, was priced significantly below an adult waffle even though the product was the same. Same waffle mix, same size, same plate, one dollar. This was a great deal for that age and stage when as much of the waffle ended up on the table and floor as in your kid's mouth.

At a certain point, my son's perspective changed on our Waffle House trips. One day, when he was about six years old, he changed his order.

On this trip, I verified his usual order.

"A kid's waffle for him," I said to our server.

"Dad, I want an adult waffle," he said.

The server stood there, her pen poised over her order pad, wondering what Dad's next move was going to be.

"The kids' waffle and the adult waffle are the same size," I said.

"But Dad, I want the adult waffle."

"It's the same waffle, John. Comes out of the same griddle my waffle does. See over there?"

I pointed to the waffle griddle, but he was having none of it.

"Dad, I want an adult waffle." He started to cry.

Our server stood there looking at me. "What now, Dad?" her eyes searched me.

At this point, in that uncomfortable moment when my kid is crying and the server is waiting, my willingness to pay shifted dramatically.

"Ok, get him an adult waffle."

I was suddenly willing to pay an adult price for that same exact waffle. If my server had told me that adult waffle prices had suddenly doubled for cheapskate Dads with crying kids, I would probably have been willing to pay that amount.

A customer's willingness to pay is subject to context as well as the geography in which they find themselves. Professional services providers, however, often miss the mark on this crucial point. A rushed completion timeline for the same work should command a premium price for the added benefit of speed, but services providers often miss this opportunity to differentiate. You should be factoring in the context and geography of your customers into your price.

Raving Fans Beg to Spend More

Raving fans are the segment of your clients who love what you do so much they will be attracted by a premium offering with benefits exclusive to them. They see so much value in your product or service that they will seek a deeper dive into what you offer. That could be a behind-the-scenes experience, special recognition as a premium customer, or other exclusive benefits not available to other customers.

Sometimes your fans are so passionate they will plead to spend more, if you're listening. Your most passionate fans see you as more than a purveyor of goods and services. They might see a cause or a mission. They see a professional with whom they have developed a meaningful relationship, someone they trust, who they know is more than competent and can deliver on even the most complex request. Often, they see more in you than you see yourself. When they do, they are willing to pay for the value they see. Listen to and study your raving fans. If you do, they could dramatically change your business.

CHAPTER 8

CRAFTING ENGAGEMENT RECOMMENDATIONS

Your engagement with a new client most likely starts with a document that details the work and tasks to be performed, as well as the fees associated with completing that work. If that's all your engagement document contains, then it's flawed, and it likely will be the cause of dysfunction in the relationship between you and your new client.

A well-written client engagement document, grounded in The Generosity Mindset, serves the client best and also allows for a tighter relationship between the transformative value your work delivers and the pricing you receive for that work.

You will notice the term I use is engagement recommendations or engagement options instead of proposals because the difference is more than semantics. As the expert, you don't propose, you recommend. Once a physician diagnoses the best course of action, do they propose a treatment? No, they recommend it, and if the patient doesn't want to follow that recommendation, the physician doesn't treat them.

You are an expert in your field. You have done that work for years for many different clients. You've seen it all, the good, the bad, and the truly ugly. You know what the problems are, and you know how to solve them. The document you've prepared offers the client a roadmap to transforming their business and their life. Why dilute all that by meekly proposing anything? You're an expert. Experts recommend.

Key Elements of Effective Engagement Recommendations

A recommendation document written and offered with The Generosity Mindset principles is the basis for a long-term business engagement and functions in three key ways to support your relationship:

- It demonstrates your expertise through a deep understanding of the client and their needs.
- It empowers a client by providing options.
- It reflects pricing that gives the client a substantial return in value relative to that pricing, and also pays you a piece of that value.

Demonstrate Your Expertise Via Your Understanding of Client Needs

The worst proposal you can submit is one that spends valuable time bragging about your qualifications, certifications, and work history. The need to cover your qualifications should be long past by this point because the client would have learned of these facts from the person who referred them to you, from your website, or during an initial call that started their vetting process.

The client must already believe you are the right person or firm for the job or you wouldn't have been asked to prepare an engagement document in the first place. So eliminate the color photos of yourself with your CV and a list of your firm's past engagements. At this point, the client doesn't care about all that, and you're either coming across as a pompous jerk or a professional who is very insecure. Either one is terrible.

When offering your engagement recommendations in writing, turn your complete attention to the client, their problems, the solutions to those problems, and an investment that will give them an outstanding return of value. The most effective way to do this is by incorporating the information you learned while listening to your prospective client during previous value conversations. Using your engagement recommendations is a sure-fire way to focus on the customer and to demonstrate that you listened to and understand their needs and values.

Call this section "Current Situation" or "Present Circumstances" or something similar. Use a simple opening paragraph, then list bullet points that relate to major points you learned in conversation with that client.

The bonus for you when you follow this methodology is that you are subtly reminding the prospect of the pain that caused them to want to work with you in the first place. In showing them what the painful present looks like, you are priming them to think about what a hopeful future can offer them as you perform your transformative work.

The Power of Options

Offering options doesn't mean a client chooses the single best-priced solution for them. You are the expert, and you recommend the best solutions available among your services options. Of course, there are different degrees of engagement.

Some clients might want the most basic of your services. Maybe it's a question of affordability or priorities. Maybe they don't want to spend the time necessary in a more comprehensive engagement. Other clients will want the top-tier option, either because they can afford it, they believe it is better than the other options, it includes everything they need to solve their problem, or because they simply like to go for the top offering every time. Options are powerful because they invite engagement. They invite a dialogue focused on problem-solving, and they position you as the expert who can solve these problems.

Your engagement recommendations should have different options that provide varying levels of engagement. Three is the optimum number of options to offer in your engagement recommendations. You do not need to name your options unless there is a clear marketing objective to do so. For most services providers, there is no clear reason, so feel free to avoid the snazzy names.

Options provide your client the feeling of control, a natural emotion most people prefer. Options also benefit you by helping to better match different clients with your service offerings they most value. Part of the psychology behind offering options rests in what psychologists call the centrality preference. This preference helps describe why, when given a choice among an array of items, most people prefer middle options versus the extremes on either end.

To put it in an everyday business context, for any given product or service, most people make a "Goldilocks" choice. They don't want the cheapest option, for fear of mediocre quality, and they might not pick the most expensive option because they either don't value the product or service highly enough or can't afford to invest that amount. In either case, the middle most often wins. If you're already utilizing options, this preference toward the middle may help you diagnose how effective your price setting is. If your clients are making choices that are tilted toward either your basic or your premium options, your pricing is off.

What if you're ready to really bring in the revenue and sell your higher-priced recommendation to your premium or "velvet rope" customers? You first must know who those customers are. They are the ones who love your product or service so much that they will pay more to get behind the "velvet rope"—an enhanced product offering or a wider suite of services—which you create.

Crafting Options

The single biggest objection I get from services providers as they develop options is that they don't know how to break down their services into a "good, better, best" framework. They understand how it can work for a products company like General Motors, which offers a Chevrolet (good), Buick (better), and a Cadillac (best). How can it work for a services business in which all services are supposedly the same?

In my experience, what is left unsaid is that all clients are getting the best of what that services provider has to offer. The deliverables for all clients, whether measured by speed, how the service is delivered, or some other measure, are all the same.

For example, my experience with bookkeepers and their respective businesses is that they largely price by the hour and the reconciliations and other monthly work gets done in order of ease of completion. If I'm a client who wants to pay an additional charge each month to receive my financials faster, I can't do that, based on the pricing model many bookkeepers have. What if, in my bookkeeping practice, I charged much more for those clients who wanted their books completed within fifteen days of month's end, a little less for those who wanted financials by the end of the following month, and even less for those who only want quarterly financials?

Speed is not the only factor you can use to differentiate your service offerings between good, better, and best. Access is another distinguishing feature. Do you only allow for email communication? How often can a client call you? Can they call only during business hours, in the evenings, or even 24 hours, seven days a week? What about how the work is performed? Are you doing everything? Do you have an assistant or a contractor doing some or all of the work? Are you outsourcing work overseas?

When you start breaking down the various scopes of work you have (or could have) for clients, and the various ways you currently (or could possibly) service them, there are a lot more possibilities for how you design a "good, better, best" framework than you might have thought possible.

From your clients' perspective, you are operating with The Generosity Mindset. You are offering them a few different possibilities for how the two of you can work together, including some options they might not have thought of. The choice is theirs as to whether they pick good, better, or best. As long as you have each of these options priced adequately (more below), you shouldn't really care which option a client chooses.

The accompanying chart can help you think about your own business through the lens of your various service attributes.

When you offer options and price them appropriately, you make it easy for your prospective client to grasp the mental math of comparing their perception of the value of extra benefits received in the enhanced option versus the added price paid. When they perceive significant added value, the upgrade decision is an easy one—in which case, you make more revenue than you would without that option. Even more important, though, you have serviced your client more effectively by giving them choices which better match the needs and values they have identified for themselves.

Service Attribute	Good	Best
Client Onboarding Process	Standard	White glove
Duration of Engagement	Short Term, Standard	Long-Term with Post Engagement Check-in
Service Package Inclusions	Basic	Comprehensive
Customization of Service	Little to None	Fully Tailored to the Client
Mode of Delivery	Standard	Premium; Fully Tailored to the Client
Speed of Service Delivery	Standard	Expedited or Priority
Accessibility and Availability	Scheduled within Normal Business Hours	24/7 with Priority Response
Client Feedback Loop	End of Engagement Only	Regular Feedback Intervals
Skills and Experience of Service Providers	Assignment to Team Members, Basic	Assignment to Most Senior Firm Member/ Owners
Interim Reporting	Oral	Oral with Supporting Documents
Reporting Frequency	Quarterly	Monthly with real-time dashboard
Post-Engagement Support	A follow-up session post engagement	Extended support with multiple follow-ups and adjustments
Outcome Guarantees	Effort-based guarantee	Defined, result-based guarantee
Warranty of Outcomes	Limited or None	Extended for predefined outcomes

An Example of Initiating Value-Based Pricing with Options

Years ago I worked with a services provider on his pricing. His "thing," I'll call it for confidentiality reasons, was a two-hour training session for $800, in addition to a few speaking engagements here and there. He was like many solopreneurs I have talked to about their pricing. He had settled on that number because it felt right. As we covered in Chapter 3 on redefining value, your pricing should not be rooted in your own feelings but in the value clients perceive in your work.

As we worked on his positioning, how he talked about value with his clients, and the value they perceived in those conversations, we sketched out three options for him to present clients using the "good, better, best" framework to craft engagement recommendations:

- "Good" (what would have been the previous proposal of $800): $1,500
- "Better": $3,300
- "Best": $5,000

We constructed these options based on the value his clients had previously identified in various services he had delivered. For the services where he lacked client feedback, we talked about the value a typical client would identify in each tier of these service offerings. Most important, we identified additional services he could offer in the "better" and "best" tiers that added more value and more revenue.

With the "best" tier, I tried to talk him up to $7,500 or even more. Again, the amounts we discussed were based on value which his client segment would perceive, and the idea that such value would represent a significant return of tangible and intangible value on their investment with him.

In re-evaluating moving his pricing to a basis in value, and introducing "good, better, best" options, my client grounded his pricing in client-perceived value. This pricing, which emerged from

The Generosity Mindset, ensured that his clients received a return on the value they perceived and identified.

When he presented these options the first time, his client selected the "better" option for $3,300. What happened, then, in terms of value for both the client and the services provider? There were demonstrable benefits for both:

- The end client received much more value than otherwise would have been the case because he was offered additional options with further value choices.
- My client received more than four times the revenue he would have received under his old pricing model.
- Landing this business at the new pricing level meant that he had three fewer leads he must convert for the same amount of revenue.
- Serving this one client, even though they selected additional options, took a lot less time and effort than servicing four clients under the old pricing model.
- He gained more time to better serve this client.
- My client opened the door to much more lucrative engagements.

Happier end client, happier consultant!

If you do nothing else after reading this book other than offer options to your clients, you will almost certainly improve your pricing and the quality of the clients you attract. I have never seen a professional services provider for whom that did not turn out to be the case.

A Small Yet Vital Detail

Your engagement recommendations for a prospective client should always have a "good until" date. An expiration does two important things: 1) helps clarify whether that client is serious, and 2) prevents you, if you're disciplined enough, from seeming too needy.

For most professional services engagements with a small- to medium-sized business, two weeks is plenty of time. If you're dealing with the decision maker of the business, and you've had a thorough value conversation followed by a review of the engagement options you prepared, then two weeks should be plenty of time for a client to either execute the agreement, engage with you over a last-minute detail or two, or explain why they might need more time.

If you haven't heard from the prospect when expiration day comes, send out an "I wish you the best" email. Tell them that since your offer to work with them expires today and you haven't heard from them, you assume that they've gone in another direction, or the timing isn't good. You thank them for their consideration and wish them the best. When you do this, the client who really wants to work with you will respond with something that amounts to, "Hold on there." They might need a few more days, or they've been legitimately sidetracked by an internal matter. They'll tell you why they haven't responded, and they'll start moving.

If you don't get a response from an "I wish you the best" email, you've most likely got a prospect who's not going to hire you. There may be any number of reasons why, but many times it can boil down to the fact that they just don't want to tell you no. They may come back down the road (in which case you'll create a new engagement letter), but for now, let them go.

With your deadline communicated clearly in writing for both the client and you to see, you are less likely to make the weak and pleading call weeks or months after hearing no response. That call is something along the lines of, "I just wanted to check in with you to see if you have any questions." This is another way of saying that you want the business badly, maybe too badly. Believe me, the client knows this all too well. If the client answers your call, they will likely tell you they've been busy or they need more time to decide. Clients with this response are generally not serious about solving the problems the two of you have identified together. Wish them well, tell them you look forward to working with them when the timing is better, and put them in your tickler file to follow up with down the road.

Do not offer to discount your services. Never budge on this. Ever. If you do, you will have blown a gaping hole right in the middle of the value you claim to offer that client. You don't adequately serve your clients by discounting the value you provide them. This idea might seem counter-intuitive, but trust me on this. Discounting will never make sense for you or the client because the rationale for your pricing should be grounded in the value clients receive. Nothing about discounts suggests value. Further, that client may be even less likely to engage you because you've given them less confidence in the value you offer.

If you call or email two weeks after submitting an engagement recommendation with some special discount or offer, you have smothered yourself with the stench of desperation and marked your initial options and deadline void. The client knows that if the expiration date in the engagement document is no good, then everything is negotiable, including pricing. Further, you might not get hired anyway because your credibility has been punctured.

It takes courage to walk away, particularly when you're new and you really need the business. What you'll find, though, is that you will be better off in the long run because clients who require you to chase them in the beginning typically end up requiring more time to service, are often needy without wanting to pay for extras or upgrades, or lack the effective communication required to maintain a solid business relationship with you.

CHAPTER 9

NEGOTIATING AND MANAGING OBJECTIONS

This chapter is deliberately misnamed.

The title refers to negotiations, but I don't consider the back and forth that happens in the time between the delivery of your engagement recommendations and when you have a signed agreement as a period of negotiation.

Negotiations most often occur between two parties who are at odds in some way, as with a business dispute, for example. If that's your definition of what happens in your early client engagements, I encourage you to rethink that idea.

To get to the point of engagement recommendations with a client, you've already had an extensive value conversation, one in which you've learned a great deal about their problems and issues, hopes and dreams. You've already determined that the two of you are a great fit. Otherwise, you wouldn't have created and prepared engagement recommendations. Both you and the client want the same thing: a successful outcome in which you deliver substantial transformative value for the client and for which you are paid based on that value.

Instead of negotiating, think of this as a continuation of the value conversation. You might not have a full understanding of client-perceived value, even though you've had what you think is an extensive value conversation followed by preparation of engagement recommendations. You may not have asked all the questions you should have, or the client may have held back on something they are particularly worried about or embarrassed by.

It is the same with the word "objections." I use the word simply because, in this context, you understand exactly what I'm referring to: it's the pushback you receive from a prospective client on price, scope of service, or some other aspect of the engagement agreement. You often think of those objections as something you must counter or overcome in some way. As with the word negotiations, the word objections feels adversarial. I invite you to rethink those words.

Objections are revelatory, not just for what the client is thinking about a potential engagement with you, but also in potentially what you have neglected to address adequately in the client dialogue. Treat so-called objections as a guidepost, as they give you the opportunity to better understand client-perceived value so you can respond appropriately.

The "It's Too Expensive" Response and What It Reveals

How do you respond to the "It's too expensive" reply? The natural reaction is to get defensive, or even worse, begin a discounting conversation with that client.

If you respond to the "It's too expensive" reply with a discount offer, you've destroyed any perception of value that client might have found in you and your services. The client quite likely will perceive that you badly need the business and that you will do just about anything to get it. If you get defensive or angry, you've also destroyed that client's perception of value, and even worse, their trust. That client may believe you have something to hide that makes you a professional they don't want to work with. Resist all these temptations.

Instead, do something that does not come naturally. Mentally thank that client. Yes, thank them. They have done you a favor. Many clients, not wanting to offend you, will give you other, often specious reasons for not wanting to move forward into an engagement. Others will disappear and "ghost" you. With these clients, you never know what the truth is.

If a client gives you the "too expensive" response, what it reveals is that you haven't had an effective value conversation. There are elements to that client's perception of value that you missed, and therefore that your recommendation summary doesn't address. What you must do at this point is engage the client in further conversation to get at what's behind their objection.

One response is simply to ask for more clarification, as in, "Could you unpack that for me?" or "Please say more on that." Another response helps address the client's needs and problems you have tried to address in your recommendation summary: "Other than price, do the services detailed here solve your problem?" What this question also helps uncover is whether your value conversation has been effective and, in turn, if your engagement recommendations are on target.

There is an exception of note here. Some prospects will have price objections simply because they love to bargain, and they think they should never pay list price. Some are bullies who are used to getting their way through intimidation and taking advantage of those who they perceive as weak. If you catch a whiff that any of these traits might be in play with a client, you must have the courage to thank them for their consideration of you and walk away. If they are problem prospects, they are certain to be problem clients.

Tutoring on Price Negotiations

I have a soft spot for tutors. Tutors are often teachers who tutor on the side to make a little extra money, and I've got an extra special affinity for teachers, since I'm married to one. Consequently, I'm delighted to help a tutor in some small way with their pricing.

Once, I visited with a tutor who had just started her tutoring business while working in sales for another company. (See why I have a soft spot for tutors? They work very hard.) She wanted to discuss her pricing because she was unhappy about her results, particularly the pushback she received from clients regarding her price. We talked about several aspects of her problem, and a big slice of what I advised was "Don't." Don't negotiate your price. Ever. Your price is what it is.

The central issue, of course, is fear. Tutors (and lots of services professionals) fear that if they refuse to negotiate, a client will walk, and they will lose that revenue. I know because I have felt that fear myself. All services professionals have. The fear is even sharper with a new business. There is a voice in the back of your head nagging you about the need for revenue. What that voice isn't telling you, though, are the problems associated with taking on too many clients at the wrong price. One of those problems is that you end up working too hard for too little revenue, and you end up resenting the very clients you got in business to serve in the first place.

It's hard to internalize that the universe is abundant, and that the right clients for you and your practice are out there, even if you turn down the one right in front of you who is badgering you about how expensive you are. I know some people read this and wonder what kind of "woo-woo" I'm on, but it's true. I've seen it play out too many times, not just for myself but for others as well.

I asked the tutor if she had ever turned down a client based on price.

"No," she said.

"You're not officially in business," I told her. I explained that you are not officially in business until you've turned down a client based on price. Once you've done that, you've passed one of several important milestones on the road to building a successful business.

A few weeks later, both of us were recruited to be photo stand-ins for a mutual friend of ours running for office.

"It happened, John," she told me, "just like you told me it would."

She'd done it. She had turned down a client based on price.

"It was hard to walk away," she said. "This lady had two children she wanted tutoring for. That's hard to turn down. She kept after me about my price. Also, there was something about her I really didn't like. I didn't have a good feeling about what working together would be like."

An important point here: Clients who bang you around about your price are often very difficult to work with. Gut feelings like the one this tutor described are ones you should pay attention to.

"I said no," she continued. "I can't tell you how hard that was. I knew I wanted that business because she has two kids, not just one. But you know, you were right. A few hours after turning her down, another client called me about my classes. This lady didn't hesitate at all when I told her the price. I got confirmation that what you told me is right!"

Yes, the universe gives. Those situations don't always work out so neatly and quickly, but it's great to hear about them when they do.

The Budget Response

Have you heard objections related to the budget? Comments such as, "We don't have the budget?"

To understand how to address this objection, you must understand what budgets really are. Budgets are not forecasts. A budget represents spending priorities. That's true for any organization, whether it's a business, a non-profit, government, or a faith community. Therefore, as an outside services provider, when you are told that there is no budget for your proposal, what you're really being told is that the outcomes your proposal will generate are not a priority. Why? It could be that you haven't done an effective job of establishing the value to that organization of what you offer. If you are working with a small business and you're told there is no budget, it's likely to be straight out balderdash.

A preponderance of small businesses I have worked with over the years operate with little to no forward-looking budget or forecast. If you are told there's no budget, then that business owner doesn't see enough value in what you offer to prioritize an investment with you. Instead of dropping your chin to your chest or shaking your head at how wrong they are, examine whether you've had an effective value conversation, one which firmly establishes the high perceived value of the outcomes you deliver.

Here is another instance in which language about priorities gets confusing: time. Let's say you're a speaker and you're trying to get on the agenda for a particular trade show or speaker series. You're told, "We don't have enough time" or "We don't have enough speaker slots to fit you in." What you are really being told is that the perceived value of your message to the audience in question is not great enough to give it precedence over other speakers and their topics.

Budgets of money and time are an allocation of resources. Resources are allocated by buyers based on the perceived value they will receive in return for investing that money and time. It is your job, as the services provider, to help establish and define that perceived value.

CHAPTER 10

INCREASING YOUR PRICE

Price increases are a normal and expected aspect of doing business. They are not something to fear or avoid.

Over time, you must increase your prices, or you will go out of business. This is simple math. If your expenses continue to rise year after year, and price adjustments are not a regular part of how you tend to your business, then you will go out of business.

Do not be anxious about price increases. Instead, embrace them. They are an essential aspect of continuing to grow your top-line revenue and to get feedback on the value you deliver to clients. To the latter point, think about what happens when you receive notice of a price increase for a service you employ? What is your first thought? Invariably, it's something along the lines of whether the service you are receiving is still worth the new, higher price. A more formal way to express it is that you are thinking about whether the value you perceive is still greater than the new price you're now being asked to pay.

When you communicate a price increase to your clients, you are creating a similar thought process for each one of them. I call it a "value decision point." They will judge whether the tangible and intangible they perceive in your services exceeds the higher price you're asking for. The most critical question you must answer for yourself when it's time for a price increase, therefore, is, "What value am I giving?"

It doesn't matter how much your costs are rising. It doesn't matter that you need a price increase to meet a revenue target for your business. Moreover, since the value in this question is the value perceived by your clients, not your own opinion of value delivered, it means that you must have had some inquiring dialogue with your clients along the way. That ongoing conversation needs to be more than skin-deep. If you're having that dialogue, then you know where you stand with the vital measure of whether your clients perceive the value they're receiving to be greater than the price they're paying. If that's the case, and only if that's the case, you can start thinking about a price increase.

Although the costs of operating your business might be a reality, the truth is, that is not a good reason to increase your prices. In fact, if your costs of doing business are climbing, so are those of other businesses, including your clients. Clients do not care about your costs, and there is no reason why they should. They are not concerned about the increased cost of support staff, travel, or office supplies. They must deal with those increases themselves, so you don't get any sympathy for that. What they care about is that the value they receive—whether tangible or intangible—is greater than the amount of the checks they write. There is nothing unreasonable about that. We all look for value more than the price we pay.

Price Increases and Client Perceptions of Value

If I told you that I had a brand-new Lexus, fresh off the assembly line, that I was willing to sell you for $1,000, what's the first question that would immediately pop into your mind?

Invariably, your first response is most likely going to be, "What's wrong with the car?"

This scenario unfolds in professional services when you price your services way too low. That's particularly true when you are relatively new in business and you haven't built a reputation in the niche or community you seek to serve. Price, in the minds of potential clients, often serves as a marketing signal. The signal may be communicating "quality" or "a lot of value" if the price is high. A price might also signal inferiority if clients see a price that is much too low relative to what they anticipated, as with the Lexus example above. Changes in your pricing, therefore, can alter the signals that pricing is sending to your chosen client niche.

A few years ago I welcomed a professional concierge, Julie Hullett, to one of my podcasts. Julie handles a wide range of personal concierge services for clients, including grocery shopping and delivery, paying bills, running errands, booking travel arrangements, and planning events. She is a godsend for the time-starved professional.

The interview we did was about her business and how she has grown, and she had much to say about how changing her pricing changed her business. I didn't bring this up. I didn't ask the question. She brought it up on her own, which is telling, I think, because Julie understood how crucial raising her prices was to not just the growth and profitability of her business, but also in attracting her best-fit clients.

"Over time, my clientele has changed," she said in the interview. "As I was running around and not making money, I realized I wasn't charging enough. Part of the problem was that I didn't understand the value of what I was offering. As I saw how much people appreciated my services, it made me think it was time to raise my prices. Naturally, I was afraid, like most business owners are when they think about a price increase.

"I overcame my fears, though, and raised my pricing. When I did that, I started getting a different and better set of clients who had different expectations. They gave me bigger responsibilities, which meant larger engagements at a higher fee."

"And because of that change in your pricing," I asked, "you attracted clients who valued what you do more?"

"Correct," she responded. "I realized the value I offered my clients. I understood that they were paying me to give them their time back. With that newfound time in their schedule, they're able to do things that are meaningful to them."

Julie had a fear of raising her fees, a natural fear that we all have. She didn't let fears or negative mindsets block her, however, from changing her business for the better. She leaned into the value clients themselves recognized in the outcomes they realized because of her work. She saw how her clients valued her services and she figured out where the clients perceived value. She began to see how high that value was relative to the low fees she charged. Seeing that gap gave her the confidence to raise her prices.

Her new pricing, she said, actually attracted better clients. Why would this be true? It's quite likely that some clients may have been interested in her services early on, but they had the same reaction as one might have to the offer of a brand-new Lexus for $1,000: It was too good to be true.

When you understand where clients perceive value, it makes it much easier for you to get over the fear of raising prices. As with prospective clients, the only way you can fully grasp where your existing clients perceive value is to ask. Ask clients where they see value in your services. These "mini value conversations" do not have to be long and involved. They could be as simple as two questions: "What are you able to do now because of my work that you weren't able to before?" followed by, "What's that worth to you?"

Have these brief dialogues with your clients over time. Don't wait until you "need" a price increase. As you continue to discover the value clients perceive in the outcomes you deliver, you will have done the homework necessary to implement successful price increases.

Communicating a Price Increase

I believe it is much better to communicate a price increase personally, not through an email or a letter. You are not a major corporation with millions of customers. Unless you have a productized service like an online legal documents service with thousands of customers, you should take advantage of your smaller size, communicate personally, receive immediate feedback, and be present to immediately address concerns or misconceptions.

Whether you communicate a fee increase verbally or in writing, there are several key elements you should include. First, explain the reasoning behind the increase. That reasoning should be couched in client-perceived value and not, as referenced earlier, be grounded in the fact that your costs have risen or some other self-referential reason. Remind the client of not just the successes of the engagement, but the tangible and intangible value of that transformation. You should review the additional value you have produced in the engagement that was unexpected and unaccounted for originally.

Make sure that you give plenty of notice. Out of courtesy, you want the client to have reasonable time to make other arrangements if they decide to engage another provider. (And that may be exactly what you want a few of your clients to do, by the way.) The right length of notice is different depending on your business, but no less than thirty days is a good guideline. The notice might be as long as a quarter or even more, depending on your billing cycles, the case of change, and other factors. Be available for further questions. The client is not prepared for this conversation like you are, and they don't know, at that moment, all the questions they want to ask. If you are in person, let them know that you will proactively discuss anything else that develops.

Do not be shy about the fee increase, and never, ever, apologize. You are not sorry, so don't say you're sorry. Further, if you do express your regrets, particularly if you are in person, the client may interpret that as an opening to negotiate the increase. In this case, you may have a bigger conversation on your hands than you bargained for.

Finally, be thankful. You are grateful for that client and the relationship you've enjoyed. If they continue with you, then you certainly have that continued opportunity to serve them. If they decide to end the engagement, you have received the value that has come from working with them, you've earned revenue, and you've learned something. Express your gratitude for them.

The Intangible Benefits of Price Increases

As you consider the tangible and intangible benefits of a price increase, you might struggle with the possibility of losing a few clients. Go into the process knowing that this is a possibility, and be okay with it. The true financial impact of a price increase suggests that you will lose a few clients. Actually, some of them probably need to be wiped from your roster anyway.

Here is a quick financial quiz for you with very simple math. Are you better off in a business where you have one hundred customers at a $50 price or ninety-five customers at a price of $54?

If you guessed the latter, you are correct. Your revenue is $5,130. If you guessed the former, that's easy to understand because we are trained to believe that more clients is always better in any business.

For your own services business, that's half right. More of the clients who are better for you is the mix you are looking for.

It is ok to allow clients who are lower fee, less profitable, and more of a hassle to leave. You may not be able to service them as effectively as you did earlier in the life of your business. If that's the case, it is in their interest to seek alternatives, which you can help with. Get over the notion that more clients is always better. What's better is more of your best-fit clients.

You might think that increasing your prices could mean the end of your business. Perhaps your existing clients won't extend their contracts, customers you have quoted in the past will no longer consider you on their short list, and newer customers will balk that your prices are increasing so soon after they've signed on. You won't fear these reactions when you have drilled down on the value you deliver.

When you release the fear, you will discover that increasing your prices actually increases the perception of your practice as being legitimate and competitive. Often, larger corporate clients view a price increase as a signal that they are dealing with a legitimate business, not merely a small subcontractor. They understand that price increases are a necessary part of business. When you demonstrate your value to them, they are likely to see a price increase as simply the cost of doing business with another company they value.

Pricing as a marketing signal becomes very important. Buyers inside corporations are invariably risk adverse. They fear missing the deliverable date on the project they're working. They fear the project getting screwed up by the vendor they hire, thereby incurring the wrath of not only their boss, but the boss's boss, who comes down on both of them. Beyond looking incompetent, a bad decision could cost them a promotion or even their job. For a corporate buyer, there is value in reliability, in knowing the project will not just get done, but will be done as agreed upon and completed on time. Value comes in knowing a services provider has the resources to get and keep the project on track. There is value in experience and reputation, evidenced in other corporate engagements successfully completed.

By the way, it's true for your best-fit clients among small businesses, too. The best ones—the ones you want to do business with—don't have time to penny pinch. They have big goals, and they need professionals who can deliver. When value delivered is at the core of your decision to increase prices, you are assured that the work you do helps your clients achieve their goals. As such, you communicate that value again and again to clients. In fact, that is how you help your clients by charging more.

I once had a client whose internal processes would have been enhanced significantly by the addition of an online form. Such a form would save them time and reduce errors compared to their current process. It would save my team on time and errors as well, which would also benefit the client.

We prepared and delivered the form, and by doing so delivered "surprise and delight" value. Down the road, that's one more element of value we are able to point to when we discussed a price increase.

If I charged by the hour, I would have had no incentive to do this. I might have tried to justify the expended hours to the client in advance, to which they may or may not have agreed. Despite any efforts I might have made to explain, they may not have fully understood the value they would realize. Alternatively, I could have taken a chance, done the work, and then hoped I wouldn't have to eat the unbilled time later. When pricing by time, the decision to invest in the client becomes begrudging instead of easy.

Do you want to run a business where your pricing causes you to feel constrained and resentful, and where you are making less money than you could otherwise? Instead, wouldn't you rather own a business where you are enthusiastic about investing more in client success, which, in turn, guides them toward their aspirations faster?

---PART 3---

GROWTH IN YOUR BUSINESS WITH THE GENEROSITY MINDSET

CHAPTER 11

RELATIONSHIPS DRIVE REVENUE

The ultimate success of your business is based on the quality of your relationships with clients, strategic referral partners, and your network in general. Is this an idea you question in any way whatsoever? I doubt it is, but because the quality of your relationships is so crucial to your business success, the concept is worth exploring and reinforcing.

Your relationship with your clients goes deeper than the quality of your work and retaining them as clients. If your business is full of clients you love working for, it shows. You go out of your way to figure out how to offer additional value. Because you do that, your clients love you even more and try harder to find ways to help you by referring other clients or sending opportunities your way.

In our social media-soaked world, it's easy to confuse relational success and media success. Confusing the two can be injurious to your business, particularly if you are counting on relationship building as a cornerstone of your business. As a solopreneur services provider, you know intuitively that relationships are what has propelled your success to date.

As you think about your marketing and business development strategies, think about this quote from *How to Win Friends and Influence People in the Digital Age*: "We must first remember that today's relational successes are not measured on the scale of media—which ones to use and how many friends, fans, or followers one can accumulate. They are measured on the scale of meaning. *Become meaningful in your interactions and the path of success in any endeavor is simpler and far more sustainable.* [Emphasis mine] The reason? People notice. People remember. People are moved when their interactions with you always leave them a little better."

When you genuinely provide value to your network and your community, whether in-person or digitally, you lay the foundation for sustainable success in your practice. You are recognized as a professional of value, and that is infinitely more impactful on your business than the momentary thrill of a viral dancing video.

Building Relationships Through the Rule of Reciprocity

Real relationships transcend anonymous downloads, views, and connection counts. Meaningful interactions can be regular social media posts that leave your followers a bit better for reading, a personal card you send, helping someone's kid with a school project in your area of expertise, or sending a meal during someone's low point in life. These meaningful interactions, genuinely offered without "gotchas" or strings, deepen relationships and widen your circle of influence. That circle of influence, in turn, will give back to you.

Here's where the rule of reciprocity, which we discussed in Chapter 2 on The Generosity Mindset, kicks in. When you genuinely seek to give to others by assisting them in their own journey and celebrating them and their work, and you do all that without expectations of a quid pro quo, you trigger the desire for reciprocity in others. Your clients will seek to help you in ways that you can't begin to imagine.

The rule of reciprocity is so powerful that its pull overcomes short-term self-interest, one's own needs, and even cultural differences, time, and geography. One powerful example Dr. Robert Cialdini offers in *Influence* is a gift that Ethiopia made to the people of Mexico in 1985 after a devastating earthquake. What made this gift so surprising and unexpected was that Ethiopia was arguably the most impoverished nation in the world at that time. Years of drought and civil war had fostered a situation in which thousands were dying of starvation and disease. Despite a myriad of their own problems, however, the government of Ethiopia sent aid to earthquake victims in Mexico.

Upon further research, Cialdini found the rule of reciprocity as the motivation for this unexpected gift: Ethiopia remembered a gift that Mexico had made fifty years earlier. When, in 1935, Ethiopia was invaded by Italy, Mexico sent aid to help the struggling country defend itself. This gift was so important that Ethiopia remembered.

Do you want to be remembered similarly? Of course you do; all of us want to be remembered such that we will receive assistance in our own journeys. This type of reciprocity is not demanded or expected. On the contrary, this powerful rule of reciprocity is triggered when you give first.

Your giving and the value you share must be offered without expectation. You cannot give with one eye on what you "deserve" or with the expectation of a quid pro quo. Otherwise, you are not planting seeds of reciprocity, but seeds of resentment.

If you build relationships by seeking to serve first, you will be seen as a professional of value. When that is your reputation in the community or niche you seek to serve, that community will organically and naturally give back to you in powerful ways that will help you build your business.

Trust is Consistency Over Time

As with any relationship in your life, consistency is key in business relationships. You cannot game consistency. You either show up or you don't. You show up at your industry group or chamber events or you are absent. You either regularly serve the group you're a part of or you don't. Your newsletter comes out every Friday or first day of the month or it doesn't. You either have a record of posting regularly to social media or your blog over the months and years or you don't. You either have a back catalog of podcasts or a series of webinars you can point to or you don't.

The payoff for consistency compounds and is far greater than your next monthly retainer payment. The payoff is best measured in the trust you develop by building relationships. This notion was perfectly captured in a quote by Jeff Weiner, former CEO of LinkedIn, who said that "Trust is consistency over time."

We think of trust as something we need to build with prospective clients so they will hire us. Trust, however, is much broader and deeper than just that. You must build trust with your strategic referral partners and your wider network, and there is never a point in which trust building ever stops. Further, while trust takes a long time to build, it is fragile and can be broken in an instant. Once that happens, it's extraordinarily difficult to rebuild.

Establishing a record of showing up over time takes patience and commitment. It's easy to get sidetracked. We've all been there. I certainly have. There is a huge reward, however, if you do the work to learn the customer values, show up, follow up, and go the extra mile. In all you do, be authentic and be sincere. That is what builds trust. Just as clients can smell fake, the best clients gravitate to the genuine, to what cannot be gamed or engineered. In a low-trust world, they crave it.

Making Connections

When I left corporate to start my business advisory practice, the relationships I needed to build my business were tenuous at best. I had left a corporate job at an international mega-bank, a job in which I worked with major corporate clients with global operations. I started with nothing but fresh business cards. I didn't have clients or even a reputation to draw on in my local community.

So what do you do when you start with nothing? What do you do if you're in business, but you need to deepen more relationships and freshen up your network? One specific answer to that question is to host your own podcast, which I'll cover in detail in Chapter 13. What if you don't even have that?

When you are brand new and don't feel like you have any great way to deepen relationships, go make connections between business owners. Make quality introductions. Early on in my business, I pitched my services, just like anyone would, but I made sure that I asked others what they needed in their business, who they wanted to meet, and what types of clients were a good fit for their business. Facilitating connections between your business contacts is a marvelous way to enhance relationships. This also takes practice and there are some land mines to watch out for.

At an event years ago, I ran into two people I thought would benefit from knowing each other. They were in complementary businesses, so they could possibly refer business to one another. They were both great networkers, meaning they would likely share resources and support each other's business however possible. Most important, I thought they would like each other personally.

As I introduced them, I suddenly went blank on one of their names. Now there's an awkward moment! I had just told this person that I wanted to help them by introducing them to someone they ought to know, and my brain wouldn't let the other person's name come off my tongue. Fortunately, I was saved by this individual's name tag, which seemed to call out, "Look at me; I'm here to help!" I recovered, and the introduction went smoothly. Even so, my brain and I weren't on speaking terms the rest of the evening.

One aspect of my business I particularly relish is making connections between others. For me, it goes beyond the enjoyment that comes from making a good connection. It's something more;

it's a calling. I believe that we are all better, particularly in the often lonely space of entrepreneurship and a world that is divided into red and blue, when we have a greater number of genuinely human and supportive connections with each other. That said, there is a right and a wrong way to build relationships this way.

The right way to drive revenue through relationships is by using The Generosity Mindset. Begin from a place of giving and service, and then trust that the revenue will come eventually, and probably from sources you might not have considered in the beginning. When you begin with generosity at the core of making connections, you will find that generating revenue is the least important thing in the moment. Instead, what you are going for is a demonstration of authentic caring, support, and helpfulness. You can't fake that. You certainly can't do that if the only idea on your mind is how and whether you'll make a buck by connecting people.

One way to be a memorable connector is to make it a practice, at the end of a meeting, to ask, "Who or what are you looking for today?" or "How can I be helpful to you today?" When you are at a networking event and speaking with someone, most particularly if they are relatively new to the group, ask them if there is anyone at the event they would like you to introduce them to.

Then, of course, you follow up on what you hear. You may already have that connection they are looking for, and all you need to do is the warm introduction. Alternately, you might need to do some hunting on their behalf. As you go about your days and weeks, you keep them top of mind. You might let others know, without using that person's name, that you're looking for a certain type of professional and to let you know if they have a recommendation. You never know what can come out of such efforts to connect. When you make the connection, don't figuratively stand there with your hand out, expecting an immediate favor in return. You will undercut your efforts and the trust you were building up until that point will vanish.

Be patient. Most people will remember your acts of generosity. Their value back to you compounds over time. The right people will be drawn to help you in any way they can; that's human nature. Occasionally, of course, you will find that person who thinks the world is a one-way street which leads to them. You might have offered a myriad of connections and assistance, and they've done nothing for you. Just move away from them and on to others in your network who view you as a professional of value and want to reciprocate.

Then, of course, there is the wrong way to make meaningful connections. My forgotten name faux pas above is but one. Connecting people by sending a blind, three-way email is another. The "You two should know each other. Enjoy!" drive-bys make the recipients feel like their pockets have just been picked clean, leaving them feeling used and confused. Although you may have good intentions for connecting the two people, your speedy effort comes across as doing just enough to try to score brownie points with both parties. That is not authentic, and it doesn't add value to either relationship.

To make the most of this type of connection, begin by placing a call to each party individually to let them know about the other individual you would like to introduce them to. Explain the other person's business and why you think the introduction would be beneficial. Ask their permission to connect them and let them know to expect an email after you've spoken with the other party and obtained their permission as well.

By placing those calls, several benefits naturally occur. You make a much more solid introduction because both individuals know you care enough to take the time to make a personal phone call rather than text or DM them on social media. You also avoid the embarrassment of someone's business or circumstances having changed such that this connection, which previously was a good one, really isn't anymore. Finally, you get the chance to deepen your connection with both parties by hearing about what's going on in their lives. With that, you can create a much more meaningful relationship-building email communication that benefits everyone.

For a few examples of such emails, visit www.thegenerositymindset. com/bookresources.

Reviews and Testimonials Support Good Relationships

Aside from connecting people to each other directly, helping others build their credibility and positive reputation is another act of generosity that supports strong relationships.

Whether on Google, LinkedIn, or some other platform, leaving a positive review is particularly beneficial for any business, especially B2C businesses that deal with a wide variety of customers and therefore get a wide range of reviews. Some of those reviews are gracious, others are outright grievous. Reviews say just as much about the people who leave them as they do about the business itself. That could bode well for you as you build a reputation for being generous with praise, thereby making a memorable impression on the readers of your review, as well as on the business owner.

You are particularly generous if you leave a positive review for that business owner who doesn't have many reviews. In their case, one negative review can bring down the average to a middling point they don't deserve. Your positive words can offset that one negative review and turn the tide of their reputation.

Your reviews and testimonials should be truthful, based on your own experience, and specific. Those "Tony the Tiger" reviews (They're great!) are better than nothing, but details, which reveal your review to be informed and familiar with the operations of the business, are even better. Just as some negative reviews are uncalled for, positive endorsements and testimonials without any basis in fact aren't useful either. The most effective testimonials demonstrate a true knowledge of the person or business being endorsed.

CHAPTER 12

MARKETING AND BUSINESS DEVELOPMENT

For solopreneurs, the line between marketing and business development is thin. Marketing comprises an array of activities that you engage in to build awareness, showcase your expertise, and engage with potential clients. Such activities include creating and maintaining a website, publishing blog posts and white papers on your website, posting on social media, sponsorship of networking events, giving presentations, writing articles for industry publications, or sending newsletters. Very broadly speaking, marketing for your business is more abstract, in that you are creating an identity and building a brand.

For solopreneurs, business development is identifying and closing new business opportunities, whether from new clients, referrals from strategic partners, deepening relationships with existing clients, or forming strategic partnerships that generate new clients. For lower middle-market companies and larger, there are distinct differences between marketing and business development, usually entire departments devoted to each. As a solopreneur, you may not see much difference in the two, or at the least, you see them as two sides of the same coin.

It Starts with Service

The most effective marketing and business development you can do starts with serving others. If you do that, you become a professional of value in their eyes. You establish yourself as not only trustworthy, but also as memorable. Ideally, you become the first consultant or bookkeeper or attorney someone thinks of when they need your services or know someone who does.

Here is what serving first looks like: One day, I received an unsolicited call from Essie Escobedo, the founder of Office Angels. Essie had a suggestion for a new client opportunity for me. That was the entire reason for the call. She had no other agenda. She wasn't trying to sell her service in any way or use the call as a pretext for something else that benefitted her. It was obvious that Essie had been thinking about my business in a strategic, not a superficial, way. One that revealed her default operating system as rooted in service. This behavior is typical with Essie, which is why her business has grown and prospered over the years. Yes, Essie is known, liked, and trusted, but all of that is triggered by her practice of putting service first.

It seems counterintuitive, and maybe even hard, to stay in a service-first frame of mind, particularly if you are new in your practice or struggling to make it go. It's easy to dismiss and say that it works for Essie or some other person, but it won't work for you because your circumstances are different. Yet if you make it a practice to serve first in your business, you will not only stand out, but your business will blossom over time. "Know, like, and trust" starts with service, and service is the lead-in for effective business development.

"People don't like to be sold, but they love to buy," says sales guru Jeffrey Gitomer. This concept should be so liberating for professional services providers that some should walk outside and scream at the top of their lungs with delight. Gitomer's statement is my answer to a services professional who said to me during a conversation about their business development, "John, it's easy for you. It's terrifying for me. I'm an introvert and I hate selling."

Sales is not about high-pressure or scripts or closing techniques. Sales and business development do not involve conversations that are a breathless rush to craft an angle on how to jam a prospect's square peg into the round hole of what you offer. Sales, particularly in professional services, is about helping people get to a place they long for in their business or life. It's about conversations that explore what's best for the client, regardless of whether it results in a ding for your cash register or not. It's about honesty in telling clients what they need and don't need, even if what they don't need involves what you do. If that is how you approach sales and business development, then I don't have to tell you that you'll be successful in your practice, because you already are.

What about that extrovert-introvert binary that so many people love to talk about? Some of that is just malarkey that's used to make introverts feel enough shame about themselves that they will buy a book or a course. I would argue that if you want to pick one or the other, introverts might be much more innately equipped with necessary business development skills, like listening and empathy, which are necessary for adopting a heart for service as you interact with the world.

If you think you have to be a "salesperson" with all the associated stereotypes that roll around in your head, you do not. Just go serve people. Sales is service. That idea ought to be liberating. You are in the professional services business after all.

Reconsider Your Marketing Mix

Do you really need a website? This question may seem like a straw man I'm setting up for you, but it's not. As a solopreneur, you are not Proctor & Gamble. You are not a major consumer products company that needs enough reach in your marketing to attract millions of customers so you can make next quarter's earnings and satisfy Wall Street. Yet, many solopreneurs make marketing decisions as if they were P&G. They spend more than is needed on a website or on search engine optimization so they will be found on Google. They spend much more time, energy, and money on social media marketing than is necessary. Their efforts are weighted too heavily toward marketing, and not enough to the relationship building involved in business development.

One of my clients, Jeff Bump, is an authority in a very specialized field: the intricacies of cement plant management, processes, and operations. Having left corporate several years ago, he is a solopreneur consultant, doing what he loves as an independent owner of his own business. I know absolutely nothing about Jeff's specialized knowledge, but I know he is an authority for one reason: I see his invoices and his numbers. (My firm prepares his financials.)

If you didn't understand his industry, you would think that his firm's name, Calcination & Comminution Consulting Services, was the most marketing unfriendly name he could create. On the contrary, he selected the name with great care to appeal to his highly narrow niche of clients, cement plants. Jeff abbreviates the name to C3S for his DBA, which is significant because C3S is the main strength component in concrete (cement) and is very easily recognized in the cement industry.

Jeff has no website. Although Jeff has a LinkedIn profile, he has never posted on LinkedIn. He has no other social media presence. It wouldn't surprise me if has never heard of TikTok or Clubhouse or SEO or sales funnels. Jeff would scream with laughter if I asked him about his personal brand.

When I asked him to come on my podcast and talk about his work, his response was, "Why do I need to do that?" (I was secretly relieved, by the way, because I'm not sure I'd know what to ask!) Needless to say, I haven't wasted my breath asking him about my team helping him start his own podcast. He doesn't need one.

Jeff is doing nothing that fits the marketing playbook for the typical professional services provider. Even so, he enjoys an extraordinarily successful practice. So what gives? Jeff understands that relationships are what drives his business, and he does what's necessary, every day, to initiate and deepen those relationships. Because of his success in building those relationships and doing excellent work for his clients, his business is robust and comes entirely through word of mouth.

I'm not suggesting that you need to take down your website or delete your LinkedIn account. Your marketing strategy is a continuum. Other than Jeff and a few others like him I know, most professional services providers need a website and a great LinkedIn presence. These marketing tools are mandatory, not optional.

Take a rational look not only at how your clients find you, but how that happens in your industry generally. There are a lot of marketing methods and tools available, which are essential if you sell a mass market product like dog food. In that case, you need to worry about SEO and keywords and digital ads and where you rank on Google.

Your business, however, is driven largely, if not entirely, by relationships. Your website, social media, etc. exist for one reason—to confirm the recommendation that a person has already made about you. You write blog or LinkedIn posts, articles for trade publications, or even a book for one reason: to confirm the depth of your expertise. Sure, you may have a few folks stumble across your website or a social media channel and call you. Depending on your specialty, that could be a great way to get new clients. (It also could be a way to generate cheapskate tire-kickers.) Better yet, you'll have people who turn out to be great clients find you because they have been drawn in by your blog posts or articles. They taste what you're serving up, and eventually they can't stand it any longer; they get in touch and want to learn more about you and possibly hire you.

Before you dive headlong and grab another marketing bauble being waved in front of you, think about how clients find you. Remind yourself who they are and where they hang out. Refresh yourself on what's working in your marketing strategies and what isn't. (You are tracking these things, right?)

Maybe, instead of falling victim to the bright, shiny object in front of you, you need to do more of what you already know works. For most services providers I know, that involves building and deepening relationships because unlike anything else, relationships move the revenue needle in your business.

Posting Prices and Value Propositions on Your Website

Many solopreneurs struggle with whether to list their prices on their website. They're afraid that they will underprice or overprice themselves by revealing their pricing, which could lead to a loss of business.

One way to share your pricing without posting your actual numbers on your website is simply to be upfront and let the world know you are not the cheapest provider. By using this technique, you speak to clients whose primary concern is the value they receive relative to the price they pay. (By the way, that's most clients.) With this approach, you have the first opportunity, before the client even calls you for an initial conversation, to delineate an effective value proposition.

I ran into a well-executed example in the case of Accu-Spec Inspection Services, a residential and commercial property inspection service based in Sevierville, Tennessee. First, how can you have a pricing page for property inspection, when the size and types of properties vary so widely? Owner Tom Maides wisely avoids such a mistake; you don't find prices on his website. Instead, Accu-Spec has a page titled "What to Look For in a Home Inspector." There is a discussion of credentials, code knowledge, and experience. There's also an explanation of why Accu-Spec incurs the added expense of using the latest technology—Infrared Thermography—in their inspections. As they explain, this technology, which some home inspectors do not utilize because of cost, can detect faulty circuits, missing insulation, water leaks, and air infiltration leaks that might not be discovered otherwise.

My favorite page on this website, though, is "Why Cheap Inspections Cost the Most." This page offers clear messages both to the low-price shopper and to the client looking for a reliable, professional home inspection: "The price of a home inspection, like many businesses, should not be the deciding factor when looking for a home inspector. We have heard many horror stories from past clients about their previous home inspector. Far too often the inspector missed something big that cost the homeowner big bucks, heartache, and a lot of trouble. The one common thread: They went with the cheapest inspector. Don't make an expensive mistake."

The price-shopper who reads this paragraph gets a clear message: Accu-Spec is not the cheapest home inspection service. An additional message, one which specifically resonates with a client understanding the need for a high-quality inspection, follows in the next paragraph: "Best value means different things to different people. Many home inspectors pride themselves on their ability to perform a home inspection in one hour and schedule four or more inspections per inspector per day. A thorough inspection is not possible with this kind of workload. An average home will require about three hours to complete a thorough inspection, and more than two inspections per inspector per day is not likely to contribute to a thorough home inspection. At Accu-Spec Inspection Services, Inc., our ethical standards, professional standards, superior reports, report delivery, and thorough inspection procedures enable us to provide the highest quality real estate inspection service in East Tennessee."

Accu-Spec is clearly telling clients that they deliberately under-schedule relative to their competitors. Doing so ensures they can take the time to provide the most thorough and professional home inspection possible. They are signaling quality to clients who want to purchase a superior inspection, those who find enough value in Accu-Spec's attributes to want to pay for them.

Whether or not you post prices on your website, always make sure you signal the value you provide. Clients willing to pay more for a premium offering (those you'd define as "best" in our "good-better-best" construct) are looking for an indication from you that you offer a premium tier of service.

Short of that, all clients, including those who will chose "good" or "better," are looking to receive more value, however they define it, than the price they pay. Your website, whether you post prices or not, needs to address that value.

Here is how another home inspection company, Home-Probe, Inc., presents value on their website:

"Consider the potential long-term costs of working with a lower-priced inspector when evaluating price. What can saving $200 now really cost you once you own the home? Getting your inspection fee refunded for a $5,000 issue you're now on the hook for quickly diminishes the 'deal' you got on your $400 home inspection.

A home inspection is another professional consulting practice. You are hiring a consultant to provide data and opinions about the home's systems and components. You're not really buying an inspection; you're buying a process developed over time and experience.

What if something goes wrong? Where does that leave you if an issue arises due to the inspector's failure to observe potential problems in a property?

What it comes down to is this: The inspection fee is small compared to the cost of the potential problem you'll then own." [Emphasis theirs.]

Note how Home-Probe deftly compares the "savings" in working with a lower-priced inspector vs. the cost of a potential problem a customer is stuck with after they own the house. Further, look how they emphasize that when a customer chooses them, they are hiring an expert who will deliver valuable outcomes.

Communicating client-perceived value is a foundational element of any website. You must communicate value in a way that your client niche easily understands and views as sound. Communicating the value of the outcomes you deliver is a much more important consideration as you construct or revamp your website than whether you will post your pricing or not.

Nice, Kind, and Your Services Business

As a solopreneur, your job is not to be nice. Your primary role is to deliver results for clients. The best clients, in fact, don't want nice. Their primary concern is the outcomes you can help deliver. They want you to diagnose and fix their problems, and yes, be kind while you do it. The best clients don't have time for shallow backslapping, and they are willing to pay your fees commensurate with the value you deliver.

You should always be kind, but kind and nice are two entirely different concepts. "Nice" is what Golden Retrievers are for. My Golden Retriever, Cooper, is always ready whenever I'd like the nice treatment: an uncritical bit of attention which asks nothing of me other than to accept it. "Kind" is what your best friends give you. While they accept you for who you are, your best friends are often those who will pull you aside, tell you when you're on the wrong track, and do so from a place of genuine care for your long-term best interests. As you manage relationships in your professional services practice, it's important to understand the difference between nice and kind.

Several years ago, I was invited by a local economic development official, let's call her Anne, to sit in on a meeting with an entrepreneur opening a new business concept. This project required a significant investment on his part, and this entrepreneur, who I'll call Bob, wanted feedback from several business professionals on his concept.

Bob delivered a presentation of his plans, including the market for his service, amount of investment, etc.

He went on.

And on.

And on.

I began to feel like my sole purpose, along with the others who'd been asked to join this meeting, was to serve as a potted plant, making the scene look tranquil but to stay quiet and acquiescent. Finally, I had an opening to ask a question, and then another one, and more after that. The questions I asked were about holes and inconsistencies I saw in his business plan. For some of the questions, Bob had thoughtful answers. For others, he scratched his head, took some notes, and said he would have to do further work. The exchanges were direct, yet friendly. That's what I thought, anyway.

Anne pulled me aside after the meeting and asked, "Is there something wrong with you?" I could tell by the way she asked the question that she wasn't really interested in my health and welfare.

"No, why?"

"You asked questions which bordered on rude."

"I thought we were here because Bob wanted feedback on his plans."

"All your questions were negative," she replied. "You didn't have to get into everything that was wrong."

Anne never invited me to any meetings like this again.

Several years later, Bob called me.

"I want to thank you," he said.

"For what?"

"You were the only person in that meeting who asked me any tough questions. What you asked made us think and helped us sharpen our plan. We're better off because of it."

It would have been enough if he had just called to tell me that, but he wanted to hire me for some consulting related to his pricing. He said he knew I would tell him what he needed to hear—what was good for the project—instead of just what he wanted to hear.

This guy, I thought to myself, *is going to be successful. He's a mature entrepreneur who understands that asking for feedback sometimes means receiving constructive criticism that would be vital to honing his plans.*

Anne thought Bob wanted a room full of Golden Retrievers, wagging their tails at everything he offered. On the contrary, what Bob wanted most of all was help getting to his desired outcomes, and he was willing to pay for that value. As a result, his business has been successful.

How to Get Great Referrals and Testimonials

In Chapter 11, you learned the importance of giving referrals, reviews, and testimonials as a great way to build relationships. Those same tools are necessary for you to receive as part of your own marketing and business development.

So how do you get great referrals and testimonials? For professional services providers, the answer is simple: Take on great clients. Only take clients who are the best fit for you and your practice. Those clients who you'll deliver stellar results for and who have no problem paying you for the value you deliver.

Great clients know other great clients. Your best clients want you to succeed, and they will go out of their way to refer business to you, in part because they feel invested in you. (That's part of what makes them great.) If you compromise and accept clients who are not the best-fit, then guess what profile of client they will send your way? A client who looks just like them: one who is not an ideal fit for your practice. That's assuming they refer anyone at all. They may not care. Roses refer roses. Thorns refer thorns. Want great referrals? Then take care in the clients you accept. Focus on clients who are the best fit.

When you have done superb work for your clients, and they sing your praises, use those opportunities to aid your marketing efforts by asking for testimonials. Most solopreneurs don't have enough of them because they are hesitant to ask. That's a problem because reviews and testimonials are such a crucial piece of what prospects and referral sources look at to determine whether they want to begin a conversation with you. Don't be shy about asking. Most clients don't mind giving a testimonial. What they don't like about testimonials is actually having to sit down and write one.

The ideal time to ask for a testimonial is when a client offers a "wow" statement, such as "Wow, Tracey, the results you've achieved from this project have been phenomenal." When you hear a statement like that, simply ask the client, "Do you mind memorializing that thought in a testimonial?" They will usually agree to do it because you've caught them at a moment in which they are expressing happiness with the choice they made to hire you.

When they say yes, offer to save them time and effort by writing the testimonial for them. When you're done, let them review and edit it as they wish before you use it. You can point out to them that LinkedIn will only accept testimonials about you from others, so they have final control over what's posted. Most clients are delighted to handle testimonials in this way. You have relieved them of all the sweat involved in something they're otherwise happy to do.

The most memorable testimonials have a specific story arc with three distinct parts:

1. "Hell"—It's the reason you were hired; the ditch that the client was in before you started your work. Here's an example: "Prior to hiring Tracey, our sales team was prone to discount instead of selling based on value. The marketplace viewed us as a commodity."

2. "Stairway to Heaven"—This part of the story is what you did to get the client out of the ditch you found them in: "Tracey's sales training and coaching gave our team a fresh perspective on the value we offer clients."

3. "Heaven"—It's the bliss that the client now enjoys because of your work: "Tracey's program led to a 30% increase in sales during the first year alone."

Here is the complete testimonial: "Prior to hiring Tracey, our sales team was prone to discount instead of selling based on value. The marketplace viewed us as a commodity. Tracey's sales training and coaching gave our team a fresh perspective on the value we offer clients. Her program led to a 30% increase in sales during the first year alone."

This testimonial is memorable and effective because it's specific about what happened because of the engagement. It addresses, head-on, what clients are looking for when they hire you: results. Testimonials with demonstrable outcomes at their core speak from the point of view of perceived client value, and those endorsements will be much more compelling as a result.

Some clients will insist on writing their own testimonial, and many of them never deliver on this promise. Those who do will not, invariably, follow the formula for a great testimonial. You will end up with something like, "Sally is a wonderful person and has been so effective in implementing her program in our company." Here you have a gracious endorsement, but it lacks punch and therefore memorability.

Whenever such testimonials come your way, you should be grateful. Always. Any testimonial, solicited or unsolicited, is a gracious gift to you. It takes both thoughtfulness and time to write one. If the testimonial you receive falls short of beaming with authenticity and specificity, however, don't be shy to ask your client for a refresh, or to approve your revised testimonial. Remember, their testimonial, viewed by others, is a reflection on them as well as on you, and you want it to be the best it can be.

CHAPTER 13

PODCASTING: THE SUPER-CHARGED VERSION OF THE GENEROSITY MINDSET

I believe that most high-ticket professional services practitioners should have their own podcast. As a solopreneur, you know your practice will be successful if you continue to build and deepen relationships important to your work. If built, those relationships will lead to revenue for your practice. If you agree, then you should have a podcast.

If you believe in The Generosity Mindset, you are 90% of the way to having a podcast that serves as a reliable marketing engine for your business. I'm not only a very active podcaster myself, but I work with other professional services firms, helping them plan and produce their podcasts, using that show to build their businesses. This work was not part of my strategic plan when I started my business advisory practice. It came along later, in a way that brings to mind the story of entrepreneur Victor Kiam.

Back in 1979, Victor Kiam's wife bought him his first electric shaver. That same year, he purchased Remington Products, a personal care products company whose offerings included electric razors. He made a fortune turning the company around. The company, which had lost $30 million in the three years prior to Kiam's purchase, made money the first year and ultimately earned Kiam a fortune. Kiam became recognized in the wider public as the TV spokesman for Remington's shaver. His catchphrase, "I liked it so much, I bought the company," made him famous in the mind of the public and was a significant factor in the Remington turnaround.

My experience with podcasting, while hardly at the scale of Kiam's, has a similar story arc. I liked the product so much, I bought the company, you might say.

Early in 2016 I was introduced to Mike Sammond, the Gwinnett County, Georgia, studio partner of Business RadioX®. Based in Atlanta, Business RadioX is a national business podcast network, operating through local studio partners like Mike who carried the BRX brand, produced business podcast content, and paid a license fee to post it on the network.

Mike had been successful with his studio in Gwinnett County, one of the biggest counties in metro-Atlanta. The Business RadioX network owners, Lee Kantor and Stone Payton, encouraged Mike to open a BRX studio where I live in the North Fulton County region, a tech-heavy, rapidly growing area north of Atlanta. Mike decided to do it, but was looking for someone who, in his words, "Knew everyone in North Fulton," to be his sidekick, who would use their existing network to open doors faster than would otherwise be the case. We got connected and the North Fulton studio of Business RadioX was launched in May 2016.

Lee and Stone advocated for local studio partners like Mike to start a "house show," a podcast aimed at the local business community. The thinking behind this idea is that most businesses don't have a place to tell their story and share their successes. Major media doesn't cover business in any depth anymore, unless there's a disaster or a scandal. Even local media, assuming they have business coverage, can be slanted toward businesses that advertise with them.

By serving as the "Voice of Business" in a local area, a **BRX** studio partner fills a gaping void in the market. Over time, as more and more business owners, executives, and leaders are featured on the show, that studio partner becomes a trusted center of influence in the local market.

With this model, it's always free to come on a show. There is no "pay to play" arrangement. Shows are never put behind a paywall, so they're always free to listen to. In the Business RadioX world, shows are never archived or removed. A business owner always has a link they can point back to that they can use in their marketing. Through this work, consistently applied over time, a studio partner introduces local businesses to the power of a podcast. Organically and naturally, business owners come back to that local studio partner to help them launch their own podcast. This model is The Generosity Mindset put into practice in the world of podcasting. Give to the tribe you want to serve, and that tribe will give back to you.

The first "North Fulton Business Radio" show was released in May 2016. Over the next couple of years, we posted about a hundred shows featuring roughly two hundred fifty guests. We had firmly established our brand in the market. Two years later, Mike decided two studios was one too many for him. He had recently married, and the studio in Gwinnett continued to grow. His plate was overflowing. Mike made me an offer to assume ownership of the studio, or otherwise he would shut it down. This decision presented a complicated calculus.

I already had an existing business advisory practice that kept me quite busy. I had a decision to make which essentially revolved around the idea of whether podcasting fit my brand. I could take over a podcast studio that was essentially break-even, so my costs were covered. The question for me was whether a podcast would integrate with my existing practice. If so, then it was an easy decision. I also questioned whether being host of my own podcast delivered enough value back to my existing business that I could advocate that other professional services providers like me should also have a podcast. The answer to both questions was a resounding yes. So I made a Victor Kiam decision: "I liked it so much, I bought the company."

The Three-Question Test on Whether You Should Have a Podcast

There is a great deal involved in starting and maintaining a successful podcast. Before you take the leap, it's important, as with any other marketing tactic, to do your homework and not make an impulsive decision.

Here are three questions to use as a guide:

- Is your business a high-ticket, B2B professional services practice?
- Do clients for your business/vertical do a lot of research before they buy?
- Is your perceived authority an important aspect of your marketing?

Answering yes to all three of these questions lands you squarely in the camp of yes, so you should host a podcast. Let's analyze each answer.

Is your business a high-ticket, B2B professional services practice? If the answer to this question is yes, and I presume it is if you're reading this book, then you should have your own podcast. To be clear, let me define "high-ticket." In using this term, I'm referring to businesses for which the lifetime value of a client is typically five figures ($10,000) or more.

To determine the lifetime value of a client, take the total amount of revenue you generate from a client during their relationship with your firm. That revenue may result from one long engagement or a series of projects or consultations you've had. Make this calculation for every client, both past and current. Determine your average revenue per client, their frequency of purchase, and their lifespan as a client. I prefer to include the value of referrals I receive from clients, which I think makes the lifetime value of a client even more accurate. (You can only do this, of course, if you're tracking who has referred business to you.)

Consider the hypothetical case of Jane the Bookkeeper. Jane determines that her average revenue per client for bookkeeping services is $600 per month. Her clients pay her monthly, so that's the frequency of purchase. The average client lifespan, based on her own track record and what she sees in her industry, is ten years.

In Jane's case, the lifetime value of a client is:

Average Monthly Revenue ($600) *times*
Frequency of Purchase (12 times/year) *times*
Client Lifespan (10 years) *equals*
Lifetime Value of a Client of $72,000

Jane the Bookkeeper, therefore, qualifies as a high-ticket services provider.

The primary way Jane or any other high-ticket B2B professional services provider builds their business is through relationships. There is a direct correlation between the growth in high-quality relationships a solo or small professional services firm experiences and the overall growth in the business itself.

Properly executed, a podcast deepens existing connections and opens the door for brand new relationships in a low-key, elegant manner. There is a profound difference between using interruption marketing or social media to sell your service versus shining the light on someone else (your ideal clients, referral partners, and prospects) on your show, allowing them to talk about themselves and their business, and giving them a piece of content they can point to with pride and use in their own marketing.

Do clients for your business/vertical conduct significant research before they buy? The more complex and higher price of the product or service, the more likely it is that a prospective client will do a lot of research to understand the source and depth of their issues. They will take time to develop an understanding of what to look for in the ideal services provider to solve those problems. For example, a business owner with a complicated business and personal tax return, who is also looking for business advisory services, is highly likely to do extensive research on a services provider, even if that professional has been referred by a trusted third party.

A podcast builds authority and allows someone to get to know you, understand how you think, and consider what it might be like to work with you in a way a blog or website cannot reveal.

Is your perceived authority an important aspect of your marketing? A high quality, consistent podcast is an ideal authority builder for professional services providers. A podcast allows you to showcase your expertise in a direct and engaging way. The consistency of a podcast over time illustrates commitment to your audience and their needs, which builds trust, trust which only deepens as the library of back episodes grows.

Further, as a former local broadcast news anchor once said to me, "Whoever is behind the mic in the middle of a city (in his case) or a particular group or industry, is viewed as a figure of authority in that region (or group). If you own the mic, then you're at the center of it all."

I once ran into a person I had known in my local business community for a number of years. He told me that he loved the work I was doing on my show and complimented me on all the superb guests I'd had. As my chest puffed out hearing all these accolades, he added, "I really need to listen to it sometime." (I remind myself of this story when I need a humility check!)

That story illustrates for me how much authority I had in the mind of that business colleague, and many more like him who aren't so candid, simply because I am recognized as the host of an established podcast. For those who listen, podcasts create a sense of intimacy between listeners and the host. Over time, listeners feel like they get to know their favorite hosts. As one listener of my podcast said to me when we first met in person, "I knew you before I knew you."

One illustration of the authority value you can build as a podcast host comes from a 2023 study jointly conducted by MAGNA's Media Trials unit and Vox Media. In the study, they concluded that podcasters are now more influential than traditional influencers: " . . . 75% of listeners say they value podcasters' influence more than they value the influence of social media influencers (15%) and TV/movie celebrities (10%)—meaning that podcasters have effectively de-throned the original influencers." That's quite an overwhelming gap in favor of podcast hosts and the influence they wield.

In the press release announcing the survey results, Edwin Wong, SVP for Insights and Innovation at Vox Media, remarked: "By its nature, listening to podcasts is one of the more intimate media experiences and it stands to reason that people will form strong attachments with their favorite hosts, but we were surprised at the deep level of connection and trust that listeners feel for their favorite hosts."

Other interesting findings in the survey included:

- 79% of listeners consider podcast content as being superior to content on social media.
- 80% of listeners say podcast hosts "feel like a friend."
- 72% of listeners listen to podcasts for self-actualization (personal growth, motivation, self-improvement, inspiration).
- 75% of listeners say they have changed their minds based on something they once believed in because of podcast hosts.
- Podcasts topped both YouTube content and social media when listeners identified the best sources of "in-depth information" and "exposure to current topics/conversations."

The Generosity Mindset Model to Format Your Podcast

If you thoughtfully and systematically apply The Generosity Mindset to your podcast, you will move the revenue needle in your business. When you format your podcast around others using The Generosity Mindset, it will benefit you in specific ways you can measure, both directly and indirectly. The biggest difference in results among my clients directly relates to this factor.

There are essentially two different formats for a business podcast:

1. **The "guru" format:** This format is all about the host and the knowledge the host shares. One of the best examples is Seth Godin's *Akimbo* podcast. Seth Godin is an extraordinarily popular marketing authority with a sizeable following built largely on a series of successful books. When he introduced his podcast, Godin already had a huge following that naturally gravitated to his show.

    To guarantee success with a "guru" format, you must already be recognized widely as a guru. Even then, there are plenty of widely recognized authorities who do not have a podcast. Further, your return on investment of time and money into your podcast will be unclear. Statistics, like the number of downloads, have limited utility to measure actual listeners. Unless clients share that they learned about you from your podcast, the evidence of the success of your podcast will largely be anecdotal and difficult to tie to a hard dollar revenue.

2. **The interview format:** The other end of this podcast format continuum is an interview format. In this case, the focus is not on the host and the host's knowledge and authority, but on the guests. The spotlight is meant to shine on the guests and

highlight them and their brand. The interview podcast format is a stellar way to implement The Generosity Mindset in your marketing. The Generosity Mindset is not just in the interview itself, but in the entire way you handle yourself as the podcast host.

Some podcasts can have a format that is a mix of both, so podcasting is not a binary, either/or choice. However you choose to conduct your podcast, remembering your business case for doing so and consistently incorporating a The Generosity Mindset will help lead you to success.

Imagine you have a prospective client you would like to develop a relationship with, in the hopes, of course, of that relationship developing into a business engagement. You have any number of options to contact that prospect. You can reach out directly to them with a cold call. You can put them on a mailing list. You can connect with them on LinkedIn and hope they will see enough of your content to think they might need you. All these traditional ways to market are either awkward or take a long time to pay dividends.

On the other hand, you can make it about the prospective client, contacting them as host of your show. You let them know that you have identified them as an ideal guest for your podcast, and you would like to have them talk about themselves and their business. Who doesn't appreciate an opportunity to talk about themselves and get the word out about their business? It is an elegant, non-threatening way to open the door for hard-to-reach prospects. Your introduction to that prospect is not as a pushy salesperson. The focus is not on you and whatever your service is. On the contrary, you are offering a generous gift for them and their business. This model works most effectively if you have a clear sense of your "best-fit" potential clients as well who your best strategic referral partners are.

As you think about the guests for your podcast, break them down as follows:

- "Ones"—Clients (particularly your "best-fit" clients and those clients who refer business to you) and "best-fit" prospects.
- "Twos"—Strategic referral partners.
- "Threes"—Nice-to-haves, but they don't really move the revenue needle in your business.

If you center your guest list around "ones" and "twos" and use that formula to serve that group of people, you will naturally initiate and deepen relationships with them.

Here is one way to think about the return on your podcast investment, using The Generosity Mindset formula.

First, you must know the lifetime value of a client to your practice, which we discussed earlier. Let's say your show airs monthly and you decide to feature two to three guests per show. You will end up with 24 to 36 guests each year. To keep the math simple, we'll keep it to 30.

Out of the 30 relationships you will either have initiated or deepened because of your podcast, how many do you think you can convert into a client relationship? Further, for those strategic referral partners you've had as guests, how many referrals will you receive from them that convert into paying clients? Three? Two? What if you can only get one out of 30? The odds are heavily in your favor that you will, and if so, the return on invested time and money is quite sizeable. For our hypothetical bookkeeper Jane, just one client a year at a lifetime value of $72,000 makes the effort wildly worth it.

Notice a very important piece of this exercise that's missing, and it's the place where most people start when evaluating a podcast: audience. Most of the services providers who come to me asking about a podcast are concerned about the size of the audience they can build, who will be listening, whether those listeners will be prospective clients, how they will know they're listening, and so forth. The Generosity

Mindset model for a podcast I'm advocating does away with all of those considerations and concerns.

When I celebrated our 500th episode of "North Fulton Business Radio," two of my guests were two of my podcast host clients, Bill McDermott, a profitability coach and host of "ProfitSense," and Anthony Chen, a financial advisor and host of "Family Business Radio."

Here's what Bill said during that show about the results he has had from following The Generosity Mindset method in his own podcast: "As a professional services advisor myself, the way it started and the way that it has turned out has really been interesting and incredibly beneficial. . . . The North Fulton Business RadioX show that I do has become the linchpin of my marketing plan. The reason for this is that the show builds relationships. Those relationships, for me, have become clients. When I look at my ROI of the cumulative effect of that business, it's hugely rewarding."

Anthony was quite succinct in his appraisal of the results he's enjoyed: "Being a financial guy, I wouldn't keep doing it if it wasn't working."

AFTERWORD

IT'S A JOURNEY

Years ago, while having lunch with a close friend of mine—someone I consider to be on my unofficial board of directors—I sought his advice on one of those "fork in the road" decisions I had to make. I can't remember exactly what it was, but what I remember vividly was the guidance he gave me.

"Do what makes your heart sing."

If thinking about a meeting with a client makes your heart sing, then that client is the right one for you. If the thought of that meeting makes your heart sound like my five-year-old grandson banging on the piano, then it's time to reassess and do something about it. It might not be that client's fault, by the way. It might be yours for having taken them on to begin with.

Let's expand the lens a bit wider. You might be captivated (and maybe imprisoned) by the idea of scaling your business into thousands of customers generating millions of dollars in revenue. Maybe you see everyone else doing it, and you feel pangs of inadequacy over where you are in your journey. By the way, what you've blown up into "everyone else" is actually a small minority. You have confused a lot of those people whose social media presence you envy—striking graphics, cool videos, and lots of likes—with their revenue. They aren't the same.

You put the big firm in your rearview mirror because you don't want to be saddled with difficult clients with corporate demands that are ruining your life. You went out on your own because you wanted to do the work you love. You want to go all out for clients you adore, sprinkling value all over them. They, in turn, love you back because of the transformative work you do for them.

Now that you have made the jump, why are you doing anything other than what makes your heart sing? Why are you in client relationships that make you unhappy? (And incidentally, the client might secretly be miserable as well.) Maybe you're taking on business that isn't a great fit because you have some artificially inflated notion of where you should be in your headlong quest to scale your business.

Let me say this very plainly: There is nothing wrong with a "lifestyle business." Don't be shamed into thinking otherwise. Anyone who looks down on your lifestyle business is a jerk you don't need to listen to. There is also nothing wrong with chasing big goals and scaling your business. If that is what makes your heart sing, go with it.

Wherever you are in your own unique journey, don't forget that the most effective way to scale your business is to change your pricing. This is not my opinion. It's an accounting fact. It works for lifestyle businesses and for businesses wanting to scale. If you make addressing your pricing a regular part of your management practice, you'll have a business that "makes your heart sing."

When I coach services providers on diagnosing and communicating value, engagements options, and pricing, they naturally reflect on previous clients and situations that they would have handled differently.

They tell the story, and it usually ends with a comment like, "I was so stupid" or "That was so dumb."

After reading this book, you have most certainly reflected on similar stories and situations in your own business when you handled a client poorly or significantly undercharged. Some of these mistakes might have been costly to you.

It's easy to reflect on what you should have done and to beat yourself up, or to think about how much the wrong mindset has cost you. Please don't do that. What I ask of you (I'm instructing you, actually.) is to not judge yourself. Give yourself grace and let it go. Instead of thinking of those situations as stupid mistakes, attach some other name. I refer to them as the tuition I paid to learn a better way. Paying tuition to learn is a natural part of our lives as professional services providers.

It's one reason why I use the journey metaphor in this book title and the rest of my work. You are on a journey. You will always be learning and improving, and you will never get it quite right. There is no magic formula that will give the right answer for all situations. Positioning, branding, communicating with prospects and clients, and pricing are all more art than science.

Moreover, clients and how they perceive value change. Learning how to diagnose client-perceived value is never ending, as no two clients are exactly the same. Even if they were, you're not the same. You have grown and developed as an entrepreneurial professional. Your services have and will evolve over time. If nothing else, technological change will see to that.

Finally, your own personal goals for your business and for your life generally will grow in different directions. Life happens, as they say, and you will decide to transition your practice in different ways.

You are on a journey in which you never quite reach the destination.

That's the way it is, not just for you, but for me and every other solopreneur.

It's a journey. Look with wonder on that journey. Marvel at where you were and the obstacles you've overcome. Look at this opportunity-filled world with generous eyes.

Enjoy the journey!

ABOUT THE AUTHOR

After a three-decade career in investment management, investment banking, and strategic advisory, John Ray formed Ray Business Advisors, a business advisory practice, in 2013. John's services include advising solopreneur and small professional services firms on their value, their positioning and business development, and their pricing. His clients are professionals who are selling their expertise, such as consultants, coaches, attorneys, CPAs, accountants and bookkeepers, marketing professionals, and other professional services practitioners.

In his other business, John is a show host and producer and owns the North Fulton (Georgia) studio of Business RadioX®. John and his team specialize in working with B2B professionals to create and conduct their own podcast using The Generosity Mindset Method: building and deepening relationships in a non-salesy way which translates into revenue for their business.

John is the host of *North Fulton Business Radio* and *The Price and Value Journey. North Fulton Business Radio*, the longest-running podcast in the North Fulton region of Georgia, features a wide range of business and community leaders. *The Price and Value Journey* is devoted to solo and small firm professional services providers and covers issues such as pricing, value, and business development. John has hosted and/or produced over 2,200 podcast episodes.

John and his wife, Dr. Monica Ray, a dedicated teacher with twenty-eight years in education, are grateful for their blended family of five children, five grandchildren, and five pets.

John is a deacon in the Episcopal Diocese of Atlanta.

ACKNOWLEDGMENTS

I have read the acknowledgements by other authors who talked about how their book was the product of a team, not just their own individual effort.

I fully understand these statements in a way now that was impossible before. Yes, my name is on the front cover, but the front cover of the book you are holding only exists because of the indispensable help of others.

My wife Monica has supported and encouraged me in ways that I cannot even begin to acknowledge in any adequate way. If there is any one person I would point to to say that this book would not exist without them, it would be her.

My editors, Anita Henderson and Karin Crompton, are fabulous. Their guidance, corrections, and challenges have made this book readable and coherent. If there are any parts of the book in which you found that not to be the case, it's entirely due to me, certainly not to Anita and Karin.

Thank you, Essie Escobedo, Julie Hullett, Gregg Burkhalter, Bill McDermott, Anthony Chen, and Jeff Bump, for allowing me to mention you by name in this book. All of you are superstars in your field of expertise and your stories will help all who read them, just as knowing each of you personally has aided me in my journey.

My beta readers offered tremendously helpful suggestions which made the book much better than it would have been otherwise. I am grateful to Gregg Burkhalter, the Rev. Ashley Carr, Darlene Drew, Essie Escobedo, Julie Hullett, Lee Kantor, Bill McDermott, Katie Moore, Stone Payton, and Stephanie Sokenis.

My friend Soumaya Khalifa, who serves as both President and CEO of Khalifa Consulting and Executive Director of the Islamic Speakers Bureau, reviewed my explanation of generosity in the Muslim faith in Chapter 2. She not only brought clarity to that passage, but her friendship and support have been invaluable.

My Business RadioX colleagues Lee Kantor, Stone Payton, Mike Sammond, and Karen Nowicki live The Generosity Mindset every day. I'm grateful for these fantastic business partners and the support and encouragement they are always ready to offer.

I have a team of superb professionals who work alongside me to deliver exceptional value to the clients we work for. I'm extraordinarily grateful for Zonya Denham, Mildred Denis, Arlia Hoffman, Angi Shields, and Cynthia Steinmetz.

Finally, I'm grateful to my clients, present and former, who entrusted me with guiding them on a portion of their respective journeys, and to the supporters of my work, all of whom are too numerous to name here. Each of you, in your own way, contributed to this book.

Printed in Great Britain
by Amazon

46044050R00119